THROUGH THE
DUTCH AND BELGIAN CANALS

PHILIP BRISTOW

D1425221

NAUTICAL

© Philip Bristow 1988

First published in Great Britain by
Nautical Books
An imprint of A & C Black (Publishers) Ltd.
35 Bedford Row, London, WC1R 4JH

Through the Dutch Canals first published in 1974
Through the Belgian Canals first published in 1972

ISBN 07136 5760 X

By the same author

Bristow's Book of Yachts
Through the French Canals
Down the Spanish Coast
French Mediterranean Harbours
Through the German Waterways

Filmset and printed in Great Britain by
BAS Printers Limited, Wallop, Hampshire

Acknowledgements

I am indebted to many Departments of the Netherlands and Belgian Governments for the facts and figures that they have kindly made available to me; to the Koninklijke Nederlandsche Toeristenbond, and particularly to Mr. J. F. J. Koens, for kindly permitting the reproduction of their splendid maps and charts; to Mr. B. V. Voskuil of the ministerie Van Verkeer En Waterstaat for help and information regarding the Deltaworks; to Mr. van den Bosch, Director of the Netherlands National Tourist Office and to Miss A. J. M. Schneider of the National Bureau Voor Toerisme, The Hague, for her kindness and patience.

I am also grateful to both the Netherlands and Belgian National Tourist Offices for permission to use many excellent photographs, besides Anthony Hall and Linda Wheeler of Smile Design, Gosport, for the artwork of the maps.

Contents

1 Suitable Boats and Equipment

The most suitable boat for a cruise of Holland and Belgium would be a motor cruiser; the power and manoeuvrability of a cruiser would make for the easiest management on the big rivers of both countries.

The accent should certainly be on power rather than on sail and large enough for the dinghy to be stowed inboard, really necessary when inland waterway cruising. Dinghies in stern davits can be quite an anxiety when manoeuvring into the small spaces often left for pleasure craft in locks. Whatever type of boat you have you should find a way of stowing your dinghy on deck. To tow it behind you in these waterways would be most unwise. You need everything inboard for peace of mind and this even applies to the drive unit, outside units, in my opinion, being unsuitable for canals and locks. I have seen them caught on the sills of descending locks and am convinced that the less you have outside of your boat the less likely you are to run into trouble.

In advocating a motor cruiser as most suitable for a cruise I should qualify this by specifying a displacement cruiser. With a planing type hull you would certainly cross the open sea quicker but the speed limits of canals would be most frustrating with a hull of this type. Planing hulls are meant to plane, after all, and are only suitable for open stretches of water.

Draft is no problem in these waterways. You could take almost any boat from the London Boat Show and cruise it around most of Holland and Belgium. But when I think of draft I think of it in terms of going alongside grassy banks, tying up anywhere which really represents most of the charm of inland waterway cruising. For this purpose twin-bilge keels are better than a centre keel. (When attempting to go alongside a bank or other pleasant spot it is a simple matter to 'nose the boat in' gently to see if there is enough water, and to go smartly astern if there is not.)

Shutsjesilen.

Regarding the equipment you will need for your cruise, warps will come high on the list and an average sized cruiser of around, say, eight tons should regard as a minimum four 15 fathom 1½in to 2in.

As far as flags are concerned, a courtesy flag will be needed, of course, and a Q. You might be glad of international code flag 'G' if you find yourself in need of a pilot.

You will need fenders and motor tyres ready to hand; the fenders for your meetings with yachts and yachthavens and the tyres for alongside barges and in locks. Four large, sausage shaped fenders are the minimum; you should not use them in locks or on commercial quays for not only do they become oily and grimy themselves but they squeeze-roll the grime into your topsides when alongside.

Motor tyres are more suitable for your commercial 'contacts', preferably the smaller Mini type. Any garage will be delighted to

Nothing to spare.

give you whatever you need. Actually they take up quite a lot of room on deck so that you will probably be able to compromise with eight or ten, say one to each 8ft of waterline. In France I advocated using one motor tyre to every 4ft of waterline but because there are so many more locks in that country you leave your tyres permanently hanging over the side and out of the way. In Holland or Belgium, where you might go for days at a time without encountering a lock, you will want to bring your tyres inboard. If you take a supply of flour sacks to cover them you will be able to protect your decks to some extent. Take enough sacks to replace when needed.

You will need some planks, as long as you can conveniently stow on deck. They will serve two purposes, first to hang outside of the tyres when alongside pontoons or piles that would otherwise work their way inside of the tyres and make annoying contact with the hull, second to act as a gangplank for the times when the gap between your boat and the bank is too wide to jump.

If you take a ladder as well you can put this out to the shore first and lay the plank along it, giving you extra strength and rigidity. You will appreciate having the ladder onboard when you come alongside an otherwise unscalable wall.

Barges are often seen displaying *Te Koop* (For Sale).

There are many pleasant places to stop in these waterways but with nowhere to secure, for few of the canals are tree-lined as in France. If you take with you iron stakes, the sort you see at roadworks, with a heavy mallet to knock them in, your choice of stopping places will be multiplied a hundredfold.

You need as big a boathook as you can handle, better still two and some long poles if you can find them. Apart from the obvious boathook uses in locks you will need to rig them or the poles, to hold you off banks when you tie up alongside in just sufficient water.

A hooter or siren is essential to announce your approach to bridges and locks. We use a compressed air siren with a renewable container.

You will need several torches for the times when you return to your boat, perhaps along unlighted canal banks. You must have a riding light to rig at night if you secure in a waterway where traffic moves during the hours of darkness.

Portable containers for fuel and water are useful safeguards. Although both are widely available, the time when you run out is sure to be the time when you are miles away from the nearest supply. Filling funnels for each will almost certainly be necessary; hose we never bother to carry because it takes up so much room and is rarely of the right fitting or length. When a hose would be of value at a supply point it is usually there.

If you are determined to cruise in your sailing boat with the unstepped mast laid on deck you will need a planned-in-advance stowage on deck. Trestles at each end of the boat are simplest with the main weight of the mast resting upon a foam rubber pad on the coach roof. Remember to label each item of standing and running rigging before it is all detached.

So much for deck equipment. Below, the first item to consider is the gas supply for cooking and the refrigerator if you have one that runs on gas. You will need a continental adaptor to take Camping Gaz type bottles that are widely available in Holland, also the larger butane commercial size cylinders.

If you have a pressurised water system you should take with you a spare pump and the knowledge to fit it.

You are not often far from a town in this area and yachting and boating equipment is available everywhere plus—and this is most important—cheerful and helpful service in your own language.

2   Locks and Bridges

There is no need to be scared of locks. It is assumed that you would not be considering the trip at all unless you possessed a certain competence in handling your boat. The biggest part of this competence is concerned with stopping and starting, with

Locks are friendly focal points, such as this one at Muiden . . .

accurately manoeuvring your craft into a predetermined position which is all that lock work is.

Some of the locks in both Holland and Belgium are enormous affairs where the lock controller is unseen, though not always unheard, and the directing of the various and multiple lock chambers is done by light signals indicating Stop and Go and also which lock to enter, with loud-speaker encouragement from time to time.

In these big locks you will stay out of trouble if you avoid dithering; in other words, if you are going, GO! The hurrying barges will not appreciate your ultra-cautious approach in a lock entry where, for instance, the barge skippers know that the lock invariably stands open. Some yachtsmen approach the lock gates or shutters as though expecting to be guillotined by them. You may depend that you will not be if the lights are green for then the locks will be open in your favour.

. . . but hurrying barges will not appreciate an ultra-cautious approach.

In the busier waterways there will invariably be other traffic at the lock approaches (too much when you are in a hurry); where the lock is closed against you you should choose your temporary tying-up spot with the greatest consideration for others. It is likely that all other traffic will be bigger than you and if you secure in the middle of a jetty that a 200-ton barge could use you will have some anxious moments.

In these waterways you should show 'after you' politeness; appreciate that you are engaged in idle pleasure cruising whilst the bustling boats around you are on urgent business. You will lose nothing by this attitude, in fact the contrary will be the case. Having displayed your courtesy to others they will be likely to help you in situations that you do not understand but they do—when, for instance, you are being personally addressed in Dutch over the loud speakers. You lose nothing in terms of progress in a lock for if there is room for you there is room and you will be the smallest present.

Even though you may be the first to arrive at a lock never assume that you will be the first to enter and, for that matter, do not seek to be the first to enter even if it was possible (lock-keepers like to pack the lock *their* way and sometimes announce order of entry by name). The occasional discomforts of being last in, under the churning screws, is preferable to the harrowing experience of having the huge hoards pounding after you when you are first out.

Huge hordes pounding after you.

Before entering a lock you will obviously have ready bow and stern warps of adequate length. On entry the foredeckhand will be standing by on the foredeck with the bow warp neatly coiled and free to run (not resembling bundles of knitting), and secured inboard.

If you are entering an ascending lock she will have to climb ashore, for which purpose iron ladders are set in the quay walls; if a ladder is visible make for it to put your foredeckhand ashore on it. If a ladder is not visible because it is obscured by an earlier arrival in the lock, and if there is no-one on the quayside (which may be out of your view above), go alongside the most convenient barge.

Assuming that your foredeckhand gains the quay with your bow warp she will take it round the nearest bollard and, if the bollard is near enough and the warp long enough, pass the end of the warp back down to you for you to secure astern. This is the simplest method of controlling your position for you have only the one warp to take up on as you rise up in the water which, in filling, will be flowing by you from ahead.

If your warp is too short for a return, because the lock is too deep or the bollard too far away, your foredeckhand will secure the bow warp ashore and you will throw her the stern warp to secure also. In this case you will have two warps to look after in order to maintain your position.

It may be that you will be by the ladder in which case you can hold in your stern by the ladder without needing to get the second warp ashore. Some yachts have a hook spliced on to a short length of rope for 'ladder hooking'. Securing to the ladder is not a good idea; your warp must only be used as a slip round the rungs. If, when the water rises (invariably the moment when your attention is diverted), you have a double granny on a rung rapidly disappearing under water and a double granny straining beyond all untying possibilities round your bitts then you are in trouble. It is not much good yelling or hooting to hold the rise in a big lock because you will not be heard; in a small lock do so and the flow will be stopped, and 'reversed' if necessary.

In addition to lock ladders there are sometimes inset bollards spaced up in the lock walls, over which you can drop a slip, transferring it to the next higher bollard as you rise. The ultimate in lock luxury is the movable bollard that rises and falls with you, being recessed in a channel in the lock wall out of the way.

It is a moment of never ending fascination when your head comes up over the side of the quay wall, like a lift up into a different life and you look about for interesting things to see, invariably disappointed but eternally hopeful. Your dearly beloved foredeckhand will be there, or strolling up to assist with the forward gate, bashing together her ladder climbing mittens to remove the dirt. Canvas mittens, placed strategically, are advisable for lock work as locks, lock ladders and lock handles are often oily and grimy and this quickly spreads to your warps.

The lock gates open ahead, the barges churn impatiently and thrash the lock water into a turmoil as they move out. Stay firmly secured while all this is going on. The moment peace returns let go, assist your foredeckhand back onboard and move out.

If the unlikely happened and you were placed first in a big lock controlled by shutters instead of gates, you should not proceed out of the lock as soon as the shutters rise out of the way; wait for the light signal that will not change to green for you until any underwater mechanism is clear.

In descending locks you come in at quay level so that your foredeckhand can step ashore to take the warp around a bollard and pass it back to you. The bargees seem to be able to flip steel hawsers on and off bollards as quick as a cowboy with a lasso; it is an art that I admire and one that escapes me for whenever I try I seem to end up with a sheepshank around a lock-keeper's leg.

The warp should be long enough to reach as you go down and pay out, with the warp secured to your bow and you holding, and checking, the other end from the stern. The water will be going ahead so that the flow will be from astern of you. In deep locks have a second warp handy to bend on if necessary. In large locks, electrically operated, there is no need for your foredeckhand to remain ashore and she can descend with you. When the gates open and the hordes have gone you simply detach by pulling your warp down from around the bollard on the quay; if it should jam as it occasionally does, perhaps in a crevice at the edge of the stone lock wall, there is nothing you can do but the lock-keeper will look to see why you are not moving and will provide help.

One way or another the warp will come back down to you and you should watch the end come down; I do mean, actually watch it. From a height it falls with quite a slap as I know to my cost for I lost a splendid pipe over the side in this way, to the scarcely concealed delight, I might add, of the foredeckhand who does not altogether approve of pipes in cabins.

In the smaller locks your crew ashore will help by opening and closing and sluicing one gate while the lock-keeper does the other.

Smaller locks.

In descending locks your crew will have to rejoin at the conclusion of this splendid physical exercise and you will need to bring the boat to the bottom of the ladder for this purpose.

There are no staircase locks in this area of the size that you encounter in France where you have flights of seven. The locks in staircase locks are joined together, the inside lock gate of the first chamber being the outside lock gate of the second and so on. Having completed the lock routine in the first lock, when the gates ahead open your crew ashore carries the warp forward to the next lock as you motor slowly ahead.

Both ascending and descending it will invariably be more convenient to secure to a barge if there is one to which you can easily make fast. A raised warp and eyebrow directed at the skipper is all that is required; take a turn with your warps round his bitts and if this entails going onboard him be careful not to mark his decks. Never risk offence by offering a tip in these circumstances, but offer sweets to the inevitable barge children by all means, in fact we always carry a tin of sweets for this very purpose. Before the lock gates open ahead and while all are preparing to leave, cast off from your barge and make fast to the quay or lock wall. When your barge is ready to leave he will not want you attached to him and when the water is turbulent with churning screws you must not be drifting free. You should stop your engines in locks if others do.

Bridge keepers often leave you in no doubt regarding their expectation of payment from you although it is considered to be but a symbolic fee. They suspend a fishing rod over you; dangling at the end of the line is a wooden clog into which you place your money. Occasionally a charge is made at locks.

Locks and bridges have various light signal patterns but whatever selection greets you you can take it that all red always means Stop and that all green always means Go. Bridge lights show red or green on either side of the span through which you are intended to pass; when red is shown on either side but with white or yellow in between it means that you can pass underneath if you can. Additional red and green lights, usually sited higher up and on the centre line of the spans, indicate when the bridge is opening or closing. Whether or not you understand their exact significance, if you GO on green, STOP for red, and GO UNDER the white/yellow when all else is red you will be correct.

Your warning to a lock or swing bridge that you are approaching is three blasts on your noise making apparatus.

When approaching bridges with a number of spans, or arches, under which you can pass you will see signals on the bridges showing you which channel to take, as follows:—

2 red horizontal bars with a white stripe between.	NO ENTRY from the direction you are coming from
1 yellow diamond	Two-way traffic
2 yellow diamonds	ENTRY from your direction only (one-way traffic)

At some junctions or crossings, signals and/or notices are displayed to warn you where traffic is coming from but you can 'see over the top' in sufficient time and you, and other approaching traffic, will be going slowly, ready to observe the crossing rule where appropriate.

The height of fixed bridges from the waterline is shown in metres, painted black on white or white on black, on most bridges. To take advantage of this necessary information it is necessary to know *your* height from the waterline, in metres and exactly.

There are two exceptions to the normal types of locks on the Belgian waterways; first the lift locks at Houdeng-Goegnies on the Canal du Centre and, second, the Sloping Lock of Ronquières on the Charleroi-Brussels Canal.

Based on the invention of an English engineer named Clarke, the lift locks are not particularly unusual and may be found on other European waterways.

As the name implies, your boat goes up or down in a lift, the lift resembling a large, oblong bath tub into which you float. Gates divide the water behind you, hydraulic pressures and compensating pumping come into play and up, or down, you go; the gates pull away, the water merges and you float out.

These lifts are over fifty years old and their differences in level are:

No. 1 at Houdeng-Goegnies	15.397m
No. 2 at Houdeng-Aimeries	16.934m
No. 3 at Bracquegnies	16.933m
No. 4 at Thieu	16.933m

Some locks stand open.

(left) The Sloping lock of Ronquieres. Floating in your tank on railway lines.

They pass about thirty barges a day and entry to them is light-controlled in the usual way. No unusual regulations apply except that you must stop your engines on entry.

The Sloping Lock of Ronquières has been called the Eighth Wonder of the World; you cannot but marvel at man's ingenuity as you glide *in* your boat *in* a water-filled tank 91m long by 12m wide *up* (or *down*) an inclined 'railway' line for 1432m.

Cruising from Brussels, when the Sloping Lock of Ronquières first comes into view your initial impression is one of incredulity and disbelief. The waterway has terminated by the low tower ahead of you and beyond it lies a set of railway lines extending upwards, for a huge distance, to a skyscraper tower at the summit.

A fixed pontoon divides the channel and extends out towards you from the lower tower that is 40m high. Outwards each side from this tower extend porticos, situated over the join of the water-way and railway; with control devices for raising and lowering the end-of-the-waterway lock gate together with the end-of-the-water-filled tank shutter—drawing both up and out from the water so that passage to and from the canal into the tank is unimpeded, or lowering them into the water to make two water-tight joins. The temporary fixing together of moving tank with permanent waterway is made by hydraulic jacks.

Lights on the portico direct you, a voice may speak from nowhere. It is likely that barges will be waiting on the right hand side and you tie up behind them.

When you go forward to examine this engineering marvel it is as well to bear in mind that you are under the surveillance of the control engineer in the top tower. At that distance he will be completely out of your range of vision but you will not be out of his; the television screen on his desk will practically pick out the brand of cigarette that you are smoking.

The water-filled tank comes gliding down the railway line bearing a floating load of either one 1350-ton barge or four 300-ton barges, eases to a stop, water levels are equalized, the 'lock' gates lift and the barges leave the tank and proceed on their way to Brussels.

Lights turn green, the voice invites you to enter. When you have done so the gates come down into the water behind you and away you go, floating in your tank that is moving on 236 rollers, up the

sloping line for a twenty minute miracle ride to change your water
level by 68m.

You arrive at the top under the skyscraper tower, (it is, in fact,
125m above water level); the same type of porticos extend over the
'join'. As soon as levels and pressures have been equalized the gates
ahead of you glide up out of the water and away you go, past lines
of barges waiting to come down.

The biggest wonder of all about this wonder of wonders is that
your boat ride is free.

Work on the Ronquières Sloping Lock started in 1962 and it
took six years to build. The boat handling control is virtually in the
hands of one man, sitting high up in the tower at the top of the
inclined plane. If you wish you can visit this tower, in fact it is
quite a tourist attraction in the summer.

Locks

Dutch girls in traditional dress near Marken.

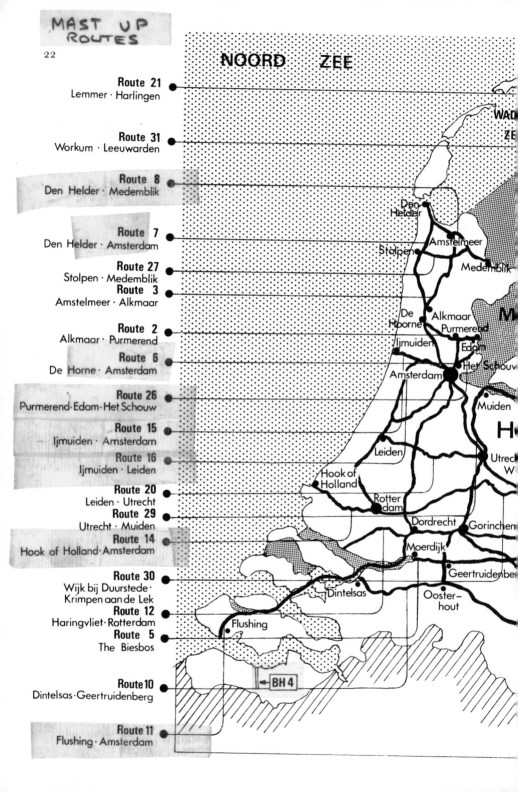

MAST UP
ROUTES

22

NOORD ZEE

WAD
ZE

Route 21
Lemmer · Harlingen

Route 31
Workum · Leeuwarden

Route 8
Den Helder · Medemblik

Route 7
Den Helder · Amsterdam

Route 27
Stolpen · Medemblik

Route 3
Amstelmeer · Alkmaar

Route 2
Alkmaar · Purmerend

Route 6
De Horne · Amsterdam

Route 26
Purmerend·Edam·Het Schouw

Route 15
Ijmuiden · Amsterdam

Route 16
Ijmuiden · Leiden

Route 20
Leiden · Utrecht

Route 29
Utrecht · Muiden

Route 14
Hook of Holland·Amsterdam

Route 30
Wijk bij Duurstede·
Krimpen aan de Lek

Route 12
Haringvliet·Rotterdam

Route 5
The Biesbos

Route 10
Dintelsas·Geertruidenberg

Route 11
Flushing · Amsterdam

Den
Helder

Amstelmeer
Stolpen
Medemblik

De
Hoorne
Alkmaar
Purmerend

Ijmuiden
Edam
Het Schouw

Amsterdam

Muiden

H

Leiden
Utrec
W

Hook of
Holland

Rotter
dam

Dordrecht
Gorinchem

Moerdijk

Geertruidenbe

Dintelsas
Ooster-
hout

Flushing

←BH 4

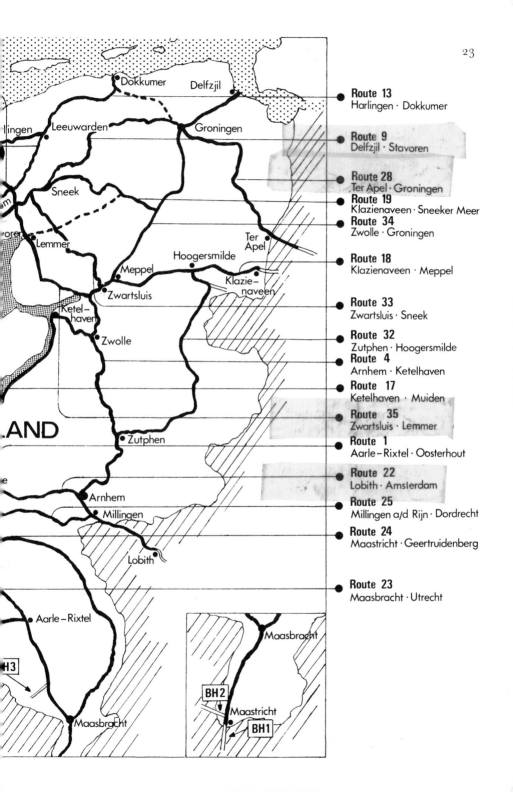

23

Route 13
Harlingen · Dokkumer

Route 9
Delfzjil · Stavoren

Route 28
Ter Apel · Groningen

Route 19
Klazienaveen · Sneeker Meer

Route 34
Zwolle · Groningen

Route 18
Klazienaveen · Meppel

Route 33
Zwartsluis · Sneek

Route 32
Zutphen · Hoogersmilde

Route 4
Arnhem · Ketelhaven

Route 17
Ketelhaven · Muiden

Route 35
Zwartsluis · Lemmer

Route 1
Aarle–Rixtel · Oosterhout

Route 22
Lobith · Amsterdam

Route 25
Millingen a/d Rijn · Dordrecht

Route 24
Maastricht · Geertruidenberg

Route 23
Maasbracht · Utrecht

3 Summary of Dutch Route Details

ROUTE 1   AARLE-RIXTEL to OOSTERHOUT via   Wilhelmina Kanaal,
Tilburg and including Eindhoven.   Beatrixkanaal

ROUTE 2   ALKMAAR to PURMEREND.   Hoornse Vaart,
Ringvaart van de Heer
Hugowaard, Ursemmer
Vaart, Beemster
Ringvaart

ROUTE 3   AMSTELMEER to ALKMAAR.   Waard Kanaal, Kanaal
Schagen-Kolhorn,
Kanaal Alkmaar-
Kolhorn

ROUTE 4   ARNHEM to KETELHAVEN via Zutphen,   Ijssel, Ketelmeer
Deventer, Zwolle, Kampen.

ROUTE 5   The Biesbos.

ROUTE 6   DE HOORNE to AMSTERDAM.   Noord Hollands
Kanaal

ROUTE 7   DEN HELDER to AMSTERDAM via Alkmaar,   Noord Hollands
Zaandam.   Kanaal, Alkmaarder,
Markervaart, Zaan,
Noordzee Kanaal

ROUTE 8   DEN HELDER to MEDEMBLIK.   Noord Hollands
Kanaal, Balgzand-
kanaal, Amstelmeer,
Sloot Vaart, Westfriese
Vaart, Ijsselmeer

ROUTE 9	DELFZIJL to STAVEREN via Groningen.	Eems Kanaal, Hoendiep, Van Starkenborgh Kanaal, Prinses Margriet Kanaal, Bergumer Meer, Meer Sloot, Biggemeer, Pik Meer, Sneeker Meer, Modderige Geeuw, Westerbrugsloot, Jelte Sloot, Heeger Meer, Fluessen, Warnser Vaart, Ijsselmeer
ROUTE 10	DINTELSAS to GEERTRUIDENBERG including Breda.	Volkerak, Mark, Mark Kanaal, Wilhelmina Kanaal, Donge, Bergse Maas.
ROUTE 11	FLUSHING to AMSTERDAM via Midaelburg, Veere, Willemstad, Dordrecht, Gouda.	Kanaal door Walcheren, Veerse Meer, Ooster Scheldt, Mastgat, Zijpe, Krammer, Zuid Vlije, Volkerak, Hollandsch Diep. Dordste Kil, Oude Maas, Noord, Nieuwe Maas, Hollands Ijssel, Gouwe Kanaal, Aarkanaal, Amstel-Drechtkanaal
ROUTE 12	HARINGVLIET to ROTTERDAM.	Spui, Oude Maas, Nieuwe Waterweg
ROUTE 13	HARLINGEN to DOKKUMER via Franeker, Leeuwarden.	Van Harinxa Kanaal, Dokkumer Ee, Dokkumer Grootdiep, Lauwersmeer
ROUTE 14	HOOK OF HOLLAND to AMSTERDAM via Rotterdam, Delft, Den Haag, Leiden, Aalsmeer.	Nieuwe Waterweg, Delfshaven se Schie, Delftse Vliet of Rijn-Schiekanaal, Nieuwe Vaart of Rijn-Schiekanaal, Zweiland and Dieper Poll, Ringvaart van de Haarlemmermeerpolder, Westeinder Plas, Ricker Plas, Nieuwe Meer

ROUTE 15	IJMUIDEN to AMSTERDAM.	Noordzee Kanaal
ROUTE 16	IJMUIDEN to LEIDEN via Spaarndam, Haarlem, Bennebroek.	Noordzee Kanaal, Zijkanaal C, Noorder Buiten Sparne, Zuider Buiten Sparne, Ringvaart van de Haarlemmermeerpolder, Dieperpoel, Norre Meer, Stoombotengat, Zweiland, Zijl
ROUTE 17	KETELHAVEN to MUIDEN via Elburg, Spakenburg.	Vossemeer, Dronter Meer, Veluwe Meer, Wolderwijd, Nuldernauw, Nijkerkernauw, Eemeer, Gooimer
ROUTE 18	KLAZIENAVEEN to MEPPEL.	Hoogeveense Vaart, Meppeler Diep
ROUTE 19	KLAZIENAVEEN to SNEEKER MEER.	Oranje Kanaal, Drentse Hoofdvaart, Opsterlandsche Compagnonsvaart, Nieuwe Vaart, Meinesloot
ROUTE 20	LEIDEN to UTRECHT via Woerden.	Oude Rijn, Amsterdam-Rijn Kanaal, Merwede Kanaal.
ROUTE 21	LEMMER to HARLINGEN via BOLSWARD.	Prinses Margriet Kanaal, Langseloot, Ee of Boomsvaart, Sloter Meer, Nauwe Wijmerts, Wijde Wijmerts, Bolswardervaart, Zeilvaart van Harlingen naar Bolsward.
ROUTE 22	LOBITH to AMSTERDAM via Arnhem, Rhenen, Utrecht, Breukelen.	Boven Rijn, Bijlands Kanaal, Waal, Pannerdens Kanaal, Rijn, Amsterdam-Rijn Kanaal

ROUTE 23 MAASBRACHT to UTRECHT via Helmond, s'Hertogenbosch, Gorinchem, Vianen.

Kanaal Wessem-Nederweert, Zuid-Willemsvaart, Kanaal Engelen-Henriettewaard, Maas, Heusdens Kanaal, Andelse Maas, Boven Merwede, Merwede Kanaal, Lek, Lek Kanaal

ROUTE 24 MAASTRICHT to GEERTRUIDENBERG via Roermond, Venlo, Heusden.

Julianakanaal, Maas

ROUTE 25 MILLINGEN a/d RIJN to DORDRECHT via Nijmegen, Tiel, Zaltbommel.

Waal, Boven Merwede, Beneden Merwede

ROUTE 26 PURMEREND–EDAM–HET SCHOUW via Monnickendam.

Purmer Ringvaart, Trekvaart van Monnickendam naar Edam, Trekvaart van Het Schouw naar Monnickendam

ROUTE 27 STOLPEN to MEDEMBLIK via Schagen.

Kanaal Stolpen-Schagen, Kanaal Schagen-Kolhorn, Ijsselmeer

ROUTE 28 TER APEL to GRONINGEN.

Ter Apelkanaal, Mussel Kanaal, Stads Kanaal, Grevelingskanaal

ROUTE 29 UTRECHT to MUIDEN.

Vecht

ROUTE 30 WIJK BIJ DUURSTEDE to KRIMPEN AAN DE LEK via Culemborg, Schoonhoven.

Neder Rijn, Lek, Nieuwe Maas

ROUTE 31 WORKUM to LEEUWARDEN.

Trekvaart van Workum naar Bolsward, Trekvaart van Bolsward naar Leeuwarden, Van Harinxma Kanaal

ROUTE 32   ZUTPHEN to HOOGERSMILDE via
Coevorden.

Twenthe, Overijssels
Kanaal, Coevorden-
Vechtkanaal, Kanaal
Coevorden-Zwinderen,
Hoogeveense Vaart,
Linthorst-Homan-
kanaal, Beiler Vaart
Brunstinger, Drentsche
Hoofdvaart.

ROUTE 33   ZWARTSLUIS to SNEEK.

Meppeler Diep, Beukers
Gracht, Belter Wijde,
Kanaal Beukers-
Steenwijk, Kanaal
Ossenzijl-Steenwijk,
Linde, Jonkers of
Heloma Vaart, Tjonger,
Pier Christiaansloot,
Tjeukemeer, Follega
sloot, Grote Brekken,
Prinses Margriet
Kanaal, Koevorde,
Westerbrugsloot,
Houkesloot.

ROUTE 34   ZWOLLE to GRONINGEN via Hasselt,
Zwartsluis, Assen.

Zwarte Water,
Meppeler Diep,
Drentse Hoofd Vaart,
Willems Kanaal

ROUTE 35   ZWARTSLUIS to LEMMER including Urk.

Zwolse Diep,
Zwanediep, Lemster
Vaart, Ijsselmeer

From BELGIUM into HOLLAND

ROUTE BH/1   LIEGE to MAASTRICHT

Meuse, Canal Albert,
Canal Ternaaien

ROUTE BH/2   NEERHAREN to MAASTRICHT.

Zuid-Willemsvaart

ROUTE BH/3   LOSEN to NEDERWEERT.

Zuid-Willemsvaart

ROUTE BH/4   GHENT to TERNEUZEN.

Canal de Ghent a
Terneuzen

You can stop almost anywhere on the Dutch canals, such as this quiet mooring near Kinderdijk.

4   Dutch Route Detail Section

WATERWAYS shown in CAPITAL letters refer to the Route that you are following . . .
WATERWAYS shown in *italics* refer to waterways leading off . . .
Diversions from the main route are shown between broken lines:—

On the Vecht.

List of Place Names—and appropriate Cruise Route Numbers

List of Place Names and appropriate Cruise Route Numbers (continued)

Alphabetical List of Waterways

Alphabetical List of Waterways (continued)

Route Detail Section 37

Route 1 Aarle-Rixtel to Oosterhout

Distance	67 kms
Number of locks	5
Minimum height above water	5m
Minimum depth of water	2m 15

*See page 136 for Map ref. details

	Kms	Locks		*Map ref
WILHELMINA KANAAL (from junction with Zuid-Willemsvaart) Connect Route 23			**AARLE-RIXTEL.** If you have wondered where all the carillons in Holland come from it is likely that they were made here. It is an interesting little town chiefly noted for the manufacture of bells. You can visit bell making factories if you wish.	11
		1		
	9		**SON ET BREUGEL**	
	7		**BATADORP**	
(L. Beatrixkanaal to Eindhoven)	2			

— — — — — — — — — — — — — — — — — — — —

BEATRIXKANAAL			**EINDHOVEN.** The town *is* the Philips Electric Company and is therefore comparatively new. The most interesting feature is EVOLUON, a permanent exhibition of scientific marvels in a mushroom shaped building. You can try to understand a computer, hear a recording of Edison's voice on a phonograph, see the person you are talking to on the telephone. EVOLUON is open from 10 to 6 every day and you can get to it easily by bus or train.

— — — — — — — — — — — — — — — — — — — —

WILHELMINA KANAAL	6		**OIRSCHOT**
		1	
	22		**TILBURG.** An industrial town with many woollen mills but quite an attractive and inviting place with beautiful parks, large mansions and a Town Hall that was once the castle of King William II.
		2	
	14		**DONGEN**

Kms	Locks	Route 1	Map ref

WILHELMINA 7 I **OOSTERHOUT.** A popular summer resort amidst
KANAAL   wooded surroundings with many fine mansions.
(from L. Mark Kanaal)
Connect Route 10

Tilburg.

Route 2 **Alkmaar to Purmerend**

Distance 31kms
Number of locks 0
Minimum height above water 2m 20
Minimum depth of water 1m 50

Kms	Locks		Map ref
HOORNSE VAART		**ALKMAAR.** The cheese town; rather a muddle of streets and waterways but quite picturesque and larger than you imagine at first sight. The cheese market is held every Friday morning, 10 to noon, from the end of April to the end of September. Weigh House 1582; Fish Market 1591; Town Hall 16thC; Municipal Museum 16thC; Grote Kerk 15thC, organ recitals Friday morning, July and August.	1G
(from junction with Noord			
Hollands Kanaal . . .			
Connect Routes 3, 7)			
(junction Schermer			
Ringvaart)	2		
Continue as RINGVAART		**HUIGENDIJK**	
VAN DE HEER			
HUGOWAARD			
	3	**OTERLEEK**	
	3	**RUSTENBURG**	

Alkmaar.

	Kms	Locks	Route 2	Map ref
LEFT on URSEMMER VAART (str. on Schermer Ringvaart)	1		**URSEM**	1 G
Join from RIGHT, BEEMSTER RINGVAART	5		**AVENHORN**	
	2		**OUDENDIJK**	
RIGHT FORK (L. fork Korsloot)	5		**BEETS**	
	2		**OOSTHUIZEN**	
	4		**HOBREDE**	
(from R. junction with Noord Hollands Kanaal . . . Connect Routes 6, 26)	4		**PURMEREND.** A small village, pretty, with convenient shops and yachts secured here and there. Church, 1358, with fine baroque organ, 1742; Interesting cattle and horse market on Tuesday mornings.	

Route 3 Amstelmeer to Alkmaar

Distance	33kms
Number of locks	2
Minimum height above water	3m 60
Minimum depth of water	2m 60

	Kms	Locks		Map ref
WAARD KANAAL (from Amstelmeer . . . Connect Route 8)			**AMSTELMEER**	1 G
	4		**WIERINGERWAARD**	
RIGHT, KANAAL SCHAGEN-KOLHORN (L. Westfriese Vaart, str. on Groetkanaal)	4			

LEFT, KANAAL	ı ı	**KOLHORN**
ALKMAAR-KOLHORN		
	4	**WINKEL**

LEFT, at 'T'	7 ı	
JUNCTION		
(R. Schager vaart)		

LEFT, at 'T'	6	
JUNCTION		
	7	**ALKMAAR**
(Junction with Noord		
Hollands Kanaal . . .		
Connect Routes 2, 7)		

Route 4 Arnhem to Ketelhaven

Distance	130kms
Number of locks	0
Minimum height above water	9m 60
Minimum depth of water	2m 80

Map ref

IJSSEL (from junction with Rijn . . . Connect Route 22)

ARNHEM. A clean and attractive city, best known in connection with the airborne attack of 1944. In the Airborne Museum in Castle 'De Doorwerth' is a permanent display devoted to the Battle of Arnhem. The city has recovered from the destruction of that time. In beautiful parks are the Netherlands Open Air Museum, a record of Holland's culture, customs, traditional costumes; a safari zoo where animals roam free; the Kröller-Müller Museum containing the largest collection anywhere of Van Gogh paintings (272 works), also Picasso, Chagall, Mondriaan.

IJSSEL

If you can manage it try to get up to Oosterbeek to see, or perhaps 'experience' would be a better word, what must be the most beautifully kept garden in the world—the cemetery of the Airborne Division.

7L

	10	**RHEDEN**	

	14	**DOESBURG**	7D

(from R. Het Zwarte Schaar)

	9	**DIEREN**	

	17	**ZUTPHEN.** A lovely old town. Sir Philip Sydney's 'Thy need is greater than mine' was uttered in Zutphen as he passed a cup of water to a dying soldier. Zutphen is rich in buildings erected by the Counts along the rivers Ijssel and Berkel. Gothic Walburgis Church; Town Hall 15thC.	

(R. Twenthe Kanaal . . . Connect Route 32)

	18	**DEVENTER.** An old Hanseatic town with ancient	

Deventer.

	Kms	*Locks*	**Route 4**	*Map ref*
IJSSEL			façades and narrow, climbing streets; a pleasant little place with everything of interest within easy walking distance. Municipal Museum, costumes, furniture and children's toys; Town Hall 16thC, books and manuscripts.	7D
	16		**VEESSEN**	

(R. Willemsvaart)   18   **ZWOLLE.** Is capital of the Overijssel Province and
(R. Zwolle-Ijsselkanaal)   greets you with beautifully laid out gardens along
the canals.
Sassen Gate 1409; St. Michael's Church 14thC;
Church of Our Lady 1463; Provincial Museum
16thC.

         15   **KAMPEN.** The imposing old gateways are a striking
introduction to Kampen. There are seagoing ships
in the harbour here; the quays are attractive with
the ancient houses amongst the warehouses of this
old Hanseatic town.
Town Hall 16thC; St. Nicholas Church 15thC;
Municipal Museum in the Brother Tower.

Kampen.

	Kms	Locks	Route 4	Map ref
			IJSSELMUIDEN	
LEFT FORK	6			
KETELDIEP				
(R. fork Kattendiep)				
KETELMEER	6			
(Junction with Vossemeer	1		**KETELHAVEN**	
. . . Connect Route 17)				

Route 5 **The Biesbos**

There is a certain charm about this roughly triangular island of islands between the Nieuwe Merwede and the Maas. The half-submerged landscape is a maze of water-channels, islands of reeds and of land, bushes, nature reserves.

The International Biesbosch Rally is held in June.

The following short routes serve as connections between other routes; they also explore the Biesbos.

MOERDIJK to GEERTRUIDENBERG

Distance	17kms
Number of locks	0
Minimum height above water	9m 70
Minimum depth of water	4m

	Kms	Locks		Map ref
HOLLANDS DIEP *(Connect Route 11)*			**MOERDIJK**	11N
RIGHT FORK, AMER *(L. fork Nieuwe Merwede)*				
	6		**LAGE ZWALUWE**	
	8		**DRIMMELEN.** Said to be the largest yacht harbour in Europe with room for 1,200 boats.	
	3		**GEERTRUIDENBERG**	
(Connect Routes 10, 24)				

Drimmelen.

Route 5
GEERTRUIDENBERG to GORINCHEM

Distance 14kms
Number of locks 1
Minimum height above water unlimited
Minimum depth of water—this route
   should only be attempted at High
   Water and preferably with a
   knowledgable guide onboard.

	Kms	Locks		Map ref
ACROSS THE AMER TO SPIJKERBOOR			**GEERTRUIDENBERG**	11N
LEFT FORK, MIDDELSTE GAT VAN HET ZAND or RIGHT FORK, BOVENSTE GAT VAN HET ZAND	3			

Geertruidenberg.

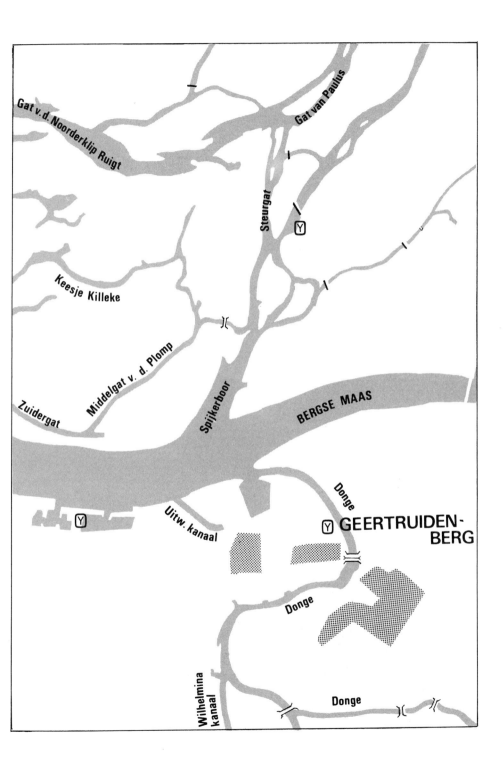

GEERTRUIDENBERG to GORINCHEM (continued)

	Kms	Locks	Route 5	Map ref
LEFT FORK,				11N
STEURGAT				
(R. fork Jeppegat)				
RIGHT, GAT VAN				
PAULUS, JOINED				
FROM LEFT BY				
NOORDERKLIP				
RUIGT	2			
LEFT, STEURGAT				
(R. Bruine Kil)	2			
(from R. Bruine Kil)	5			
(R. Kanaal Steurgat)				
		1		
			BIESBOS HAVEN	
RIGHT, IN MERWEDE				
		2	**WERKENDAM**	
			(near GORINCHEM)	
(Connect Routes 23, 25)				

Route 6 **De Hoorne to Amsterdam**

Distance	37kms
Number of locks	1
Minimum height above water	unlimited
Minimum depth of water	4m 50

	Kms	Locks		Map ref
NOORD HOLLANDS KANAAL LEFT AT ALKMAARDER (str. on Alkmaarder)	1		**DE HOORNE (Alkmaarder)** (Connect Route 7)	1 G
(R. Kogerpolder Kanaal)	3			
(L. Vuile Graft to Driehuizen)	1		**WESTGRAFTDIJK**	
	2		**OOSTGRAFTDIJK**	
(Junction L. Beemster Ringvaart R. Knollendammer vaart)	2			
RIGHT, NOORD HOLLANDS KANAAL	9	1	**PURMEREND** *(Connect Route 2)*	
(R. Dorre Ilp)	8		**ILPENDAM**	
(Junction Gouw Sloot)	3		**WATERGANG**	
(L. Trekvaart van Het Schouw to Monnickendam)	2		**HET SCHOUW**	
	6		**AMSTERDAM.** There are yacht harbours on the various waterways into Amsterdam where you can leave your boat and explore the city by bus or tram. If you are resourceful and patient you can bring your boat right into the heart of Amsterdam but it is probably easier on the nerves to 'park' outside. You may take it for granted that if you do this and explore by tram, your crew will draw attention to yachts (British flag of course),	

Map
Route 6   *ref*

AMSTERDAM (continued)
secured alongside everywhere in most desirable
locations. If you bring your boat in, after your
tenth encounter with a bridge and your twentieth   1G
encounter with a water-bus it will be suggested by
your crew that the city could have been half
explored by tram in the time already taken. You
can explore in your dinghy, of course, and you will
see many small boats doing this, but keep a
continuing note of your bearings for you will have
heard that Amsterdam is famous for its hundred
canals and thousand bridges.

However you explore, Amsterdam is an exciting
city; practically every street seems to have a
waterside setting, many tree-lined. The atmosphere
is enlivened by organ grinders extracting gay tunes
from what appear to be hoardings on wheels,
strong men in pairs pushing them everywhere.
Maritime Museum, historical ship models, paintings, prints, maps, nautical instruments. Rijkmuseum,
17thC Dutch masters; Rembrandt (the 'Night
Watch' is in a room on its own), Vermeer,
Hobbema, Potter, Steen, De Hoogh, Stedelijk
Museum, Impressionists including Delacroix,
Rousseau, Daumier, Manet, Monet, Toulouse-
Lautrec, Gaugin, Cézanne, Renoir, Degas, Picasso,
Braque, Mondriaan.

Van Gogh Museum; Tropical Museum; Memories of
the Pilgrim Fathers at the Begijnhof Almshouse;
Rembrandt's house, the Mint Tower 1620 and, of
course, the Royal Palace on Dam Square (completed
(Connect Routes   1665).
7, 11, 14, 15, 22)

Route 7 Den Helder to Amsterdam

Distance	70kms
Number of locks	0
Minimum height above water	unlimited
Minimum depth of water	3m

	Kms	Locks		Map ref
NOORD HOLLANDS KANAAL *(Connect Route 8)*			**DEN HELDER**. Quite a large place with big stores and shops. It is principally a naval town with barrack type buildings and dry dock facilities, in fact Den Helder is the principal naval base of the country. You seem to see as many warships as yachts (but do not photograph as there are signs forbidding this). The navy have their own harbours and the fishing boats have theirs; yachts moor within walking distance of the shops and there are all facilities here. Naval Museum; Aquarium.	1 G
(L. Balgzandkanaal)	4		**DE KOOI**	
	9		**T'ZAND**	
Den Helder.				

	Kms	Locks	Route 7	Map ref
NOORD HOLLANDS				1 G
KANAAL				
(L. Kanaal Stolpen-	3		**STOLPEN**	
Schagen . . .				
Connect Route 27)				
(Junction Groote Sloot)	9			
		4	**SCHOORLDAM**	

Schoorldam.

	Kms	Locks	Route 7	Map ref
	. 6		**KOEDIJK**	
(L. Hoornse Vaart)		7	**ALKMAAR**	
(L. Schermer Ringvaart)			*(Connect Routes 2, 3)*	
			DE HOORNE	
STRAIGHT AHEAD		8		
TO ALKMAARDER				
(L. Noord Hollands			*(Connect Route 6)*	
Kanaal)				
LEFT CHANNEL		4		
(R. to Uitgeest)				
RIGHT, INTO				
MARKERVAART				
		3	**MARKENBINNEN**	
LEFT INTO ZAAN		1	**WEST KNOLLENDAM**	
(R. Nauernase Vaart)				

		Map
Kms Locks	**Route 7**	*ref*

RIGHT AT JUNCTION — 1G
(L. Knollendammer Vaart)

1	**OOST KNOLLENDAM**
2	**KROMMENIE.** A small industrial town.
1	**WORMERVEER**
2	**ZAANDIJK.** An interesting little village with an antiquities museum.
3	**ZAANDAM.** Two hundred years ago this was the leading shipbuilding centre in the world. Today it is a busy industrial centre.

LEFT INTO 3
NOORDZEE KANAAL

*(Connect Routes
6, 11, 14, 15, 22)*
Amsterdam.

AMSTERDAM

Route 8 **Den Helder to Medemblik**

Distance	32kms
Number of locks	7
Minimum height above water	unlimited
Minimum depth of water	2m 65

	Kms	Locks		Map ref
NOORD HOLLANDS KANAAL			**DEN HELDER**	1 G
(Connect Route 7)				
		1		
LEFT, BALGZAND- KANAAL	4		**DE KOOI**	
		1		
Medemblik.				

	Kms	Locks	Route 8
AMSTELMEER *(R. V. Ewijcksvaart)*	6		
(R. Waard Kanaal)	3		**DE HAUKES**
RIGHT, SLOOT VAART *(L. Den Oeverse Vaart to* *Den Oever)*		I	
JOIN FROM RIGHT *WESTFRIESE VAART*	4	I	**SLOOTDORP**
	5		**MIDDENMEER**
	10	3	**MEDEMBLIK.** On the waterfront is the mediaeval Castle Radboud.
IJSSELMEER			*(Connect Route 27)*

Route 9 Delfzijl to Staveren

Distance   125kms
Number of locks   4
Minimum height above water   unlimited
Minimum depth of water   2m

	Kms	*Locks*		*Map ref*
EEMS KANAAL		1	**DELFZIJL.** Is important because it is the entry port to the Eems Kanaal. Chimneys rise out of a grey skyline, cranes overhang a small yacht harbour surrounded by what appears to be an area of waste ground; there are shops and everybody tries hard in the harbour but there is absolutely no attraction for the yachtsman here except, perhaps a Neptune Festival at Whitsun. There is also a race from Delfzijl to Borkum and back in late June. Delfzijl is mainly a shipbuilding and industrial town.	3
	14		**BOUWERSCHAP**	
(Junction L. Winschoter diep—R. Van Starkenborgh Kanaal)	12			
	1		**GRONINGEN.** A lively commercial and university	

Eems Kanaal.

Groningen.

Kms	Locks	Route 9	Map ref
		town of much interest, with barges and craft of all kinds scattered around its many quay walls. The industrial side on the waterways towards Delfzijl is as industrial as you will find anywhere but it is away from the splendid shops and markets. Maritime Museum; Natural History Museum; Niemeijer's Dutch Tobacco Museum; St. Anthony's Hospice 1517.	3

REITDIEP		**GRONINGEN**	
(Junction van	5	**DORKWERD**	
Starkenborgh Kanaal)	6	**GARNWERD**	
	8	**ROODEHAAN**	3
	12	**ZOUTKAMP**	
LAUWERSMEER			
1812.1			
(Connect Route 13)			

	Kms	Locks	Route 9	Map ref
			GRONINGEN	3
HOENDIEP		I		
	4		**HOOGKERK**	
(R. Aduarder diep)				
	I		**VIERVERLATEN**	
	5		**ENUMATIL**	
	3		**ZUIDHORN**	
LEFT INTO VAN STARKENBORGH KANAAL	2			
	4	I	**GAARKEUKEN**	
	4		**EIBERTSBUREN**	
	3		**STROOBOS**	
PRINSES MARGRIET KANAAL	I		**GERKESKLOOSTER**	2A
	8		**KOOTSTERTILLE**	
ACROSS BERGUMER MEER	2		**SCHUILENBURG**	
PRINSES MARGRIET KANAAL	5		**BERGUM**	
LEFT AT FORK, MEER SLOOT (R. Van Harinxma Kanaal . . . Connect Routes 13, 21)	4		**FONEJACHT**	
PRINSES MARGRIET KANAAL				
RIGHT AT FORK (L. to Sijtebuurster Ee) ACROSS BIGGEMEER (R. De Meer)				
ACROSS PIK MEER	7		**GROUW**	
PRINSES MARGRIET KANAAL				

	Kms	Locks	Route 9	Map ref
(Junction L. Boorne *R. Rak van Ongemak)*	3			
CROSS SNEEKER MEER *(R. to Sneek)*	7			2A
MODDERIGE GEEUW	3		**UITWELLINGERGA**	
WESTERBRUGSLOOT				
(Junction L. Geeuw *Langweerder Vaart* *R. de Brekken)*	3			
PRINSES MARGRIET *KANAAL*				
RIGHT INTO *JELTE SLOOT* *just before De Koevorde* *(Connect Route 21)*	2			

— — — — — — — — — — — — — — — — — — — —

	Kms	Locks	Route 9	Map ref
STRAIGHT ON ACROSS *DE KOEVORDE*				
PRINSES MARGRIET *KANAAL*	6		**SPANNENBURG**	
GROTE BREKKEN *(L. Follega Sloot . . .* *(Connect Route 19)*	1			
	5		**LEMMER** *(Connect Routes 21, 35)*	

— — — — — — — — — — — — — — — — — — — —

	Kms	Locks	Route 9	Map ref
RIGHT INTO *JELTE SLOOT* *just before De Koevorde*				
	5		**HEEG**	
CROSS HEEGER MEER *AND FLUESSEN*				
WARNSER VAART	19	1	**STAVEREN**	
IJSSELMEER				

Route 10 **Dintelsas to Geertruidenberg**

Distance	57kms
Number of locks	2
Minimum height above water	7m
Minimum depth of water	2m 10

	Kms	Locks		Map ref
VOLKERAK			**DINTELSAS.** A lonely outpost. The industrial	11
(Connect Route 11)			harbour area is enclosed behind gates.	
		1		
DINTEL	7		**STAMPERSGAT**	

Dintel.

		4	**STANDDAARBUITEN**
MARK			
		9	**HAZELDONK**
		10	**TERHEIJDEN**
LEFT, MARK KANAAL		2	

– – – – – – – – – – – – – – – – –

	5	**BREDA.** Former seat of the Counts of Nassau. It is a delightful experience to come ashore here, to wander amongst the attractive terraces and shops of the Grote Markt, and amongst the stalls, to an accompaniment of the 45-bell carillon. There is also

Breda.

					Map
	Kms	Locks			ref

an antique and art market. Great Church of Our
Lady 15thC Museum in the old Meat Hall 1614.

MARK KANAAL

		1		
LEFT INTO	5		**OOSTERHOUT**	K
VILHELMINA KANAAL			*(Connect Route 1)*	

FROM RIGHT, DONGE 5

GEERTRUIDENBERG

BERGSE MAAS 5
(Connect Routes 5, 24)

Route 11 Flushing to Amsterdam (Vlissingen)

Distance	180kms
Number of locks	7
Minimum height above water	unlimited
Minimum depth of water	2m 75

Locks

WESTER SCHELDE

*KANAAL DOOR
WALCHEREN*

1

*Map
ref*

FLUSHING. An attractive little town, a holiday 1803.1
resort with a fine sandy beach and promenade. It
is also a fishing port and a shipbuilding centre, the
shipyard employing many thousands. Flushing is
the only port of any size that is actually on the sea.
The statue on the promenade is of Michiel de
Ruyter who was born here. Museum, local
antiquities, model ships. Grote Kerk 14thC.

Flushing.

Kms	*Locks*	**Route 11**	*ref*

KANAAL DOOR 6   **MIDDELBURG.** Capital of Zeeland, with   1805.4
WALCHEREN   buildings recalling the days of the 17thC trading
companies. An interesting town, badly bombed in
1940. You may see traditional costumes appear at
the Thursday markets. 'Miniature Walcheren'
Exhibition from April to September.

1

7   **VEERE.** The construction of the Dam has closed
off Veere from the North Sea since 1961 and it is
becoming a leading yachting centre, a most delightful
place to be so honoured. It is one of the most
charming towns in Holland. Gothic Town Hall and
the 'Scottish Houses' Museum by the harbour;
Museum, old maps, costumes, Ming China.
The 15thC Church of Our Lady dominates the
town.

RIGHT IN VEERSE   1805.4
MEER

Veere.

	Kms	*Locks*	**Route 11**	*Map ref*
VEERSE MEER				1805.4
The channel is well buoyed in the comparatively open waters from here to the entrance to the Dortse Kil.				
	6		**ORANJEPLAAT**	
	9		**KORTGENE**	
	4		**ZANDREEKDAM**	
LEFT IN OOSTER		1		1805.1
SCHELDE, follow buoyed channels around drying banks into KEETEN continue through				
MASTGAT				1805.3
ZIJPE			**ZUID GREVELINGEN**	1807.2
KRAMMER				
ZUID VLIJE				1807.3
VOLKERAK			**DINTELSAS.** A lonely outpost indeed. The industrial harbour area is enclosed behind gates; there is a harbour here but nothing else. *(Connect Route 10)*	

ZUIDER VOORHAVEN

Willemstad.

		Map
Kms Locks	**Route 11**	*ref*

<table>
<tr><td></td><td>47</td><td>I</td><td>**VOLKERAKSLUIZEN**</td><td>1807.6</td></tr>
</table>

RIGHT IN
HOLLANDSCH DIEP

2   **WILLEMSTAD.** A pretty little harbour and a refreshing introduction to Holland after battling with barges through to Hollandsch Diep. Willemstad is a charming little fortress town with well kept ramparts and bastions. The first Protestant Church in the Netherlands is here.

9   **STRIJENSAS**

LEFT, DORDSTE KIL   3
(str. on Hollandsch Diep)

RIGHT, OUDE MAAS   9   **DORDRECHT.** A town of delightful and typically   J

Dordrecht.

	Kms	*Locks*	**Route 11**	*Map ref*

OUDE MAAS

Dutch canal vistas with houses rising directly from the water; the view you see is the best view, of the oldest and most attractive part, and you do not realise that there are new buildings too in Dordrecht until you go ashore. There are waterways everywhere. Since it is surrounded by great rivers it is no surprise to find that Dordrecht is a big shipbuilding and yachting centre.

Grote Kerk 15thC, white interior, huge organ of 3600 pipes with 10 second echo. From 17thC Groothoofdspoort Gate there are superb views over the Oude Maas. Van Gijn Museum, rare collection of antique toys. Dordrecht Museum, many old masters.

(Connect Route 25)

LEFT, NOORD   3   **PAPENDRECHT**
(R. Beneden Merwede)

     4   **ALBLASSERDAM**

LEFT, NIEUWE MAAS   3   **KRIMPEN AAN DE LEK**
(Joining from R. Lek)   *(Connect Route 30)*

RIGHT, HOLLANDS   4   I   **KRIMPEN AAN DE IJSSEL.** As you approach it
IJSSEL   appears that the huge structure ahead is a lock but it is the raised shutter of a huge storm flood barrage.

     3   **OUDERKERK AAN DE IJSSEL**

     3   **KLEIN HITLAND**

     3   **IJSSELLAAN**

     3   **MOORDRECHT**

     2   I

LEFT, GOUWE KANAAL   **GOUDA.** A town of waterways, mostly   H
(R. Hollandse IJssel)   decorative; an interesting and charming place. Principally famous for its cheese, the Cheese Market is held every Thursday morning throughout the summer. There are splendid shops and it is a lively town.

Sint Janskerk 15thC, the country's largest church; priceless stained glass. Town Hall 16thC; Weigh House 1668; Municipal Museum, mediaeval surgical instruments, old toys, early Dutch kitchens.

Gouda.

	Kms	*Locks*	**Route 11**	*Map ref*
GOUWE KANAAL	4		**WADDINXVEEN.** A pleasant little place specialising in the growing of flowering plants and shrubs.	H
	4		**BOSKOOP.** Noted for botanical gardens and roses, also for the cultivation of flowering plants and small trees, trained into shapes resembling animals etc.	
(Junction Oude Rijn) *(Connect Route 20)* *CONTINUE AS AARKANAAL*	5		**GOUWSLUIS**	
	5		**TER AR**	
RIGHT FORK AMSTEL-DRECHT-KANAAL *(from R. Kromme Mijdrecht Connect Route 20*	5	1		1
	8		**UITHORN**	1
LEFT AT FORK (R. Bullewijk), CONTINUE ON AMSTEL-DRECHTKANAAL	7		**OUDERKERK**	
	7		**AMSTEL YACHT HARBOUR** **AMSTERDAM**	
(Connect Routes 6, 7, 14, 15, 22)				

Route 12 **Haringvliet to Rotterdam**

Distance   32kms
Number of locks   1
Minimum height above water   8m
Minimum depth of water   2m 60

Rotterdam.

Route 13 Harlingen to Dokkumer Nieuwe Zijlen

Distance	47kms
Number of locks	1
Minimum height above water	2m 60
Minimum depth of water	1m 90

VAN HARINXMA KANAAL

HARLINGEN. The steamers that you see in the harbour remind you that this is quite an important sea port and a terminal for the ferries to Terschelling and Vlieland. It is the harbour for crab and mussel fisheries. Around the port are attractive quayside houses with a bewildering variety of gables. Town Hall 1750; Museum, collection of ship models.
(Connect Route 21)

Map ref
2A

Harlingen.

Kms	Locks	Route 13	Map ref
VAN HARINXMA 8 *KANAAL*		**FRANEKER.** An old town whose principal attraction is the 1775 Planetarium. It was once a famous university town. Renaissance Town Hall 1591;	2A
(R. Franker Vaart, *Connect Route 33)* 2		St. Martin's Church 1421; Grain Carriers' House 1634; Martena House 1498, with Rococco interior, is a reminder of the former prosperity of the town.	
5		**DRONRIJP**	
(L. Deinemerrak) 6		**DEINUM**	
LEFT AT FORK 2 *(R. Van Harinxma Kanaal)* 4		**LEEUWARDEN.** Capital of Friesland it is an interesting town, standing on artificial hills on reclaimed land. The Chancellery 1571; Stadhouder's Residence 1587; Weigh House 1598 (now a restaurant); the leaning Oldehove Tower 1532; Princessehof Museum, Eastern art, porcelain; Natural History Museum; Frisian Museum, intricate silverwork; Jacobin Church 1492 containing the tombs of the Frisian Nassau Rulers. *(Connect Routes 21, 31)*	

Leeuwarden.

			Map
Kms	*Locks*	**Route 13**	*ref*

LEFT DOKKUMER EE 2A

10	**BIRDAARD**

6   **DOKKUM.** A small walled town with mediaeval
street planning. Charming Town Hall 1762,
Admiralty House and Church.

RIGHT, DOKKUMER
GROOTDIEP
(L. Zuider Ee to Ezumazijl)

1

4   **DOKKUMER**
NIEUWE ZIJLEN

LAUWERSMEER   1812.1
(Connect Route 9)

Route 14 Hook of Holland to Amsterdam

Distance	99kms
Number of locks	1
Minimum height above water	unlimited
Minimum depth of water	2m 50

	Kms	Locks		Map ref
NIEUWE WATERWEG *(Europort on R.)*			**HOOK OF HOLLAND.** Situated just inside the Nieuwe Waterweg, the Hook is the principal ferry terminal with Great Britain. It is a 'day-tripper' type of resort overlooking the North Sea, the wide Nieuwe Waterweg and the refineries of Europort. You would not be interested to moor here even if there were facilities for yachtsmen.	J
	16		**MAASLUIS.** An industrial town and a big ferry crossing. You will see many barges in the creek but it is no place for a cruising yacht.	
(R. Oude Maas)		5		
LEFT DELFSHAVEN *SE SCHIE*	10		**ROTTERDAM.** Astride the most important waterways in Europe (the Rhine and the Maas), Rotterdam, second city of Holland, is the largest	

Rotterdam.

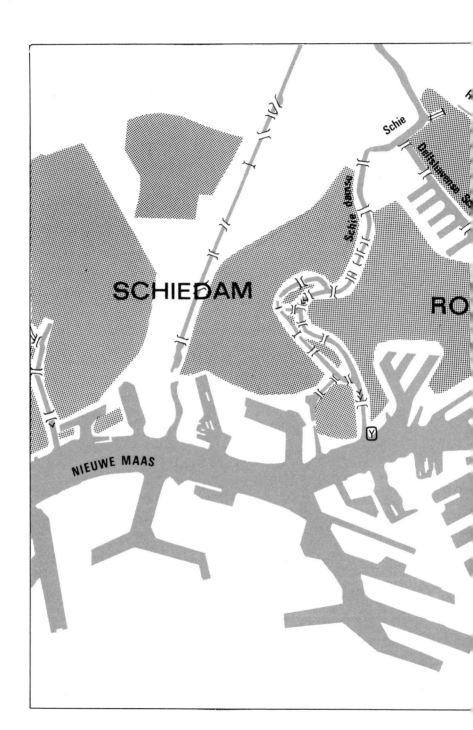

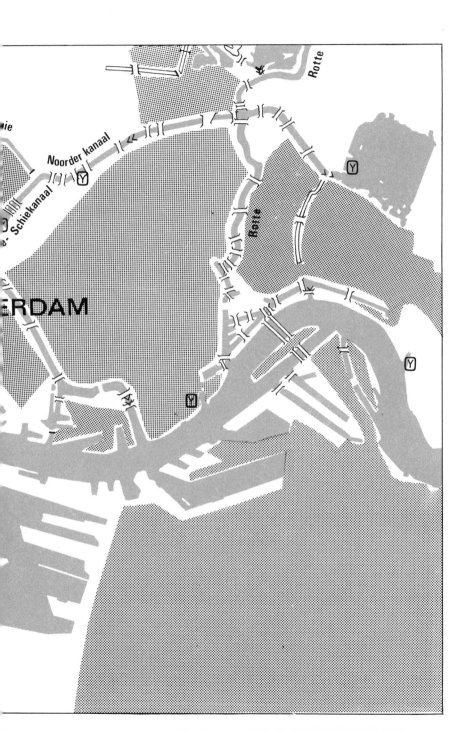

	Kms	Locks	Route 14	Map ref

Rotterdam (cont.)

DELFSHAVEN *SE SCHIE* — seaport in the world. Facilities include radar equip- **J** ment that can bring ships from the North Sea, up the Nieuwe Waterweg to Rotterdam harbour, in nil visibility. Just across the Maas the largest oil refinery in Europe is being developed. There are barge basins and yacht basins and basins *Verboden Voor Jachten*; with sixty ships and six hundred barges *per day* visiting Rotterdam it is no place for the cruising yacht. Rotterdam was destroyed by bombing in 1940 so that it is all comparatively new. The first underground railway in Holland was constructed here. Ashore and afloat all is bustle and efficiency. The *Groothandelsgebouw* is a vast shopping complex, ten stories high and 700ft long.

(Connect Route 12.)

(R. Schie—Schiekanaal)   4

RIGHT AT 'T'   1   **OVERSCHIE**
JUNCTION

4   **DE ZWETH**

Rotterdam . . . the Euromast.

	Kms	*Locks*	**Route 14**	*Map ref*
RIGHT AT FORK	5		**DELFT.** One of the most attractive towns in Holland with tree-lined canals and 16thC houses. In June the Art and Antique Dealers' Fair is held in the Prinsenhof. Vermeer was born here but the chief claim to fame of this town is, of course, its blue and white earthenware, the famous Delft Blue. In the Lambert van Meerten Museum is a fine collection of Delft pottery.	H
DELFTSE VLIET OF RIJN-SCHIEKANAAL				
(L. Trekvliet)	4		**RIJSWIJK**	
	6	1	**DEN HAAG.** The Dutch Parliament is here and all the ministries that go with it but The Hague (or Den Haag or s'Gravenhage), is not the capital; in a water conscious country Den Haag cannot compete with the capital, Amsterdam. It is a pleasant city, compact, with attractive gardens, small canals, lurching trams, palatial banks everywhere. Mauritshuis 17thC, Dutch masters; Gemeente Museum, modern art and odd looking musical instruments. Mesdag Museum, Impressionists. You should see the model (miniature), town of Madurodam.	
(L. Korte Vlietkanaal)	6			
NIEUWE VAART OF RIJN-SCHIEKANAAL	4		**LEIDEN.** Best known for its university (founded 1575), Leiden is a delightful place; the view of it as	

Leiden.

	Kms	Locks	Route 14	Map ref

Leiden (cont.)

NIEUWE VAART OF RIJN-SCHIEKANAAL

you wait for the bridge to open, the pink and white buildings, the well placed windmill, the green of grass and background trees make it the sort of typical Dutch town of your imagination. Ashore you find interest everywhere amongst the twisting streets, with music from the street organs reverberating amongst the 17thC Dutch gables. De Lakenhal Museum, old masters. General Hoefer Military Museum, weapons, uniforms. Het Molem Museum, windmills. Het Museum van Oudhem, ancient history.

(Connect Routes 16, 20) — H

(Junction Nieuwe Rijn)

ACROSS ZWEILAND AND DIEPER POLL — 9 — **BUITENKAAG**

RIGHT, RINGVAART VAN DE HAARLEMMERMEER-POLDER
(L. Ringvaart van de Haarlemmermeerpolder to Haarlem)

(R. Oude Wetering Connect Route 20) — 6 — **WETERINGBRUG**

— 2 — **LEIMUIDEN**

WESTEINDER PLAS — 2

— 2 — **RIJSENHOUT**

RINGVAART VAN DE HAARLEMMER-MEERPOLDER — 3 — **AALSMEER** is famous for its flower auction, said to be the biggest of its kind in Europe, with separate sale rooms for potted plants, cut flowers and bulbs. Most of these are brought to the auction by barge but leave by air from nearby Schipol for world-wide destinations. A guide will take you round and you will see bidders bidding by pressing buttons before them as in a television quiz game; the price and the bidder's seat number then lights up on the large clock face. — I

RIGHT INTO RIEKER PLAS NIEUWE MEER — 10

(Connect Routes 6, 7, 11, 15, 22) — **YACHTHAVEN, AMSTERDAM**

Route 15 Ijmuiden to Amsterdam

Distance	23kms
Number of locks	0
Minimum height above water	unlimited
Minimum depth of water	10m

IJMUIDEN. The locks will take the biggest ships   G
in the world with room to spare; you will be
directed to the smaller size. The entry harbour is on
the starboard side and consists of bare, high quays,
tugboats, fishing boats and a few shops ashore. This
is the largest fishing port in Holland. On the other
side of the Nordzee Kanaal is the yacht harbour in
a background of chimneys, industry, belching
smoke. But moving up the Nordzee Kanaal the
scenery soon improves.

ZAANDAM. Two hundred years ago this was the
leading ship-building centre in the world. Today it
is a busy industrial centre.

AMSTERDAM

Route 16 **Ijmuiden** (near) **to Leiden**

Distance	40kms
Number of locks	1
Minimum height above water	unlimited
Minimum depth of water	2m 50

<table>
<tr><td></td><td>Kms</td><td>Locks</td><td></td><td>Map
ref</td></tr>
<tr><td>NOORDZEE KANAAL
(10k from Ijmuiden)</td><td></td><td></td><td></td><td></td></tr>
<tr><td>RIGHT, INTO
ZIJKANAAL C</td><td></td><td>1</td><td></td><td></td></tr>
<tr><td></td><td>3</td><td></td><td>SPAARNDAM. Where the boy stuck his finger in the dike—or, at least, the legend is perpetuated by a memorial in this interesting little town.</td><td>G</td></tr>
<tr><td>RIGHT, NOORDER
BUITEN SPARNE</td><td></td><td></td><td></td><td></td></tr>
<tr><td></td><td>5</td><td></td><td>HAARLEM. A pleasant city with a fashionable shopping area around the Grote Market. If you are interested in antiques there are many shops here. Frans Hals Museum 17thC; Town Hall 13thC; St. Bavo's Church with the world famed Müller Organ, 1738, once played by Mozart.</td><td></td></tr>
<tr><td>LEFT, ZUIDER
BUITEN SPARNE</td><td></td><td></td><td></td><td></td></tr>
<tr><td></td><td>3</td><td></td><td>HEEMSTEDE. A small town, semi-industrial and with road traffic predominating; there are quite pleasant gardens but it is not of much interest to the cruising yachtsman.</td><td>H</td></tr>
<tr><td>RIGHT, INTO
RINGVAART VAN DE
HAARLEMMER-
MEERPOLDER</td><td>4</td><td></td><td></td><td></td></tr>
<tr><td></td><td>3</td><td></td><td>BENNEBROEK. The place to be at bulb time for one of the principal growing areas is here. After the first delight the view of flowers seems to dissolve into vast slabs of colour arranged with parade-ground precision. The Linnaeushof Garden has beautiful displays of flowers in season.</td><td></td></tr>
<tr><td></td><td>4</td><td></td><td>HILLEGOM in the bulb growing area; here you can see a display garden of the bulb growers.</td><td></td></tr>
</table>

	Kms	Locks	Route 16	Map ref
RINGVAART VAN DE HAARLEMMERMEER-POLDER		3	**LISSE.** A bulb growing area.	H
DIEPERPOEL (*Continuing L. Ringvaart in de Haarlemmermeerpolder*)		5	**BUITENKAAG**	
NOORE MEER				
STOOMBOTENGAT				
ZWEILAND				
ZIJL		7		
(*Connect Routes 14, 20*)		3	**LEIDEN**	

Ijmuiden.

Route 17 **Ketelhaven to Muiden**

Distance   79kms
Number of locks   3
Minimum height above water   12m 90
Minimum depth of water   3m

	Kms	*Locks*		*Map ref*
			KETELHAVEN.	E
VOSSEMEER	1			
CONTINUE IN DRONTER MEER	8	1	**ROGGEBOT**	
CONTINUE IN VELUWE MEER	10		**ELBURG.** An old harbour town. The gateway dates from 1392, the old Town Hall, originally built as a monastery, from 1300.	
CONTINUE IN WOLDERWIJD	16	1	**HARDERWIJK.** An old harbour town, pleasant and not crowded, with an academy that was once important. Dolphinarium.	
CONTINUE IN NULDERNAUW	7			
CONTINUE IN NIJKERKERNAUW	8	1	**NIJKERK**	
	5		**SPAKENBURG.** Another town in which you can see traditional costume worn by the inhabitants, and also hung out to dry across the streets. The harbour is slowly dying but shops are to hand; the Saturday afternoon market is an event.	
(L. Eem to Amersfoot)	4			
CONTINUE IN EEMMEER				
	7		**HUIZEN**	
CONTINUE IN GOOIMER				
	8		**MUIDERBERG**	
IJ MEER	5		**MUIDEN.** The well known water castle of Muiden is one of the most impressive buildings in Holland and dates from the Middle Ages. There is a ship-yard also Royal Netherlands Yacht Club.	E

(Connect Route 29)

Muiden.

Boats of many types
conveniently
berthed at Muiden.

Route 18 **Klazienaveen to Meppel**

Distance 53kms
Number of locks 8
Minimum height above water 4m 20
Minimum depth of water 1m 55

Map
ref

Kms Locks

'OOGEVEENSE VAART   **KLAZIENAVEEN**   *
(*Connect Route 19*)

4   **ERICA**
   1

3   **NIEUW AMSTERDAM.** With a name like this
you would expect to find an exciting city but it is
no more than a village street of shops lining the
water.

* There is no Waterkaart for this route.

Reflections on the Hoogeveense Vart at Erica.

Zwinderen.

Kms	Locks	Route 17	Map ref
HOOGEVEENSE VAART 14		**ZWINDEREN** *(Connect Route 32)*	
	1		
12		**HOOGEVEEN.** An industrial town in beautiful surroundings. If you hear the sound of a drum on Sundays do not leap ashore in the hope of seeing a band and marching; the stern Protestant inhabitants are being drummed to church several times in the day.	
	6		
20		**MEPPEL.** A pleasant place situated at the entrance to the moorland lakes of Beulaker Wijde and Belter Wijde. On Thursdays during July and August there is a farmers' market when Staphorst costumes are worn. The nearly Staphorst population are not exactly publicity conscious; it is forbidden by law to take photographs of this fanatically religious community.	

MEPPELER DIEP
(Connect Route 34)

Route 19 Klazienaveen to Sneeker Meer

Distance 102kms
Number of locks 12
Minimum height above water 3m 20
Minimum depth of water 1m 50

Hoogersmilde.

	Kms	Locks	Route 19	Map ref
LEFT,				
OPSTERLANDSCHE	1			
COMPAGNONSVAART			**HIJKERSMILDE**	
	2		**APPELSCHA**	
RIGHT, AT FORK	6	3	**OOSTERWOLDE**	
(L. Tjonger Kanaal)				

	Kms	Locks	Route 19	Map ref
TJONGER KANAAL			**OOSTERWOLDE**	
	18	3	**MILDAM**	
RIGHT, PIER	17			
CHRISTIANSLOOT				
TJEUKEMEER	3			
FOLLEGA SLOOT	4			
(Connect Route 9)				

	Kms	Locks	Route 19	Map ref
RIGHT, AT FORK			**OOSTERWOLDE**	
OPSTERLANDSCHE	1			
COMPAGNONSVAART	2		**DONKERBROEK**	*
	7		**KLEIN GRONINGEN**	
	13	3	**GORREDIJK**	
NIEUWE VAART	2	1	**TERWISPEL**	
(L. Buiten Ringvaart)				
	13		**OLDEBOORN**	B
	5		**AKKRUM**	
LEFT, MEINESLOOT				
	4		**TERHORNE** **SNEEKER MEER**	
			(Connect Route 33)	

* There is no Waterkaart available until OLDEBOORN.

Route 20 **Leiden to Utrecht**

Distance   53kms
Number of locks   3
Minimum height above water   2m 40
Minimum depth of water   2m

	Kms	Locks		Map ref
OUDE RIJN			**LEIDEN**	H
	2		**LEIDERDORP**	
	5		**HAZERSWOUDE**	
(L. Heimans wetering *. . . Connect Route 14)*	5		**ALPHEN AAN DEN RIJN.** Principally noted for Avifauna International Bird Park where some 10,000 birds of 400 different species are housed in gardens of exceptional beauty; tropic birds in heated glasshouses, polar birds in icy caves, ostriches and emus on lovely lawns, penguins, toucans, pelicans.	
(Junction L. Aarkanaal, *R. Gouwe . . .* *Connect Route 11)*	2		**GOUWSLUIS**	
	4		**ZWAMMERDAM**	
	3	1	**BODEGRAVEN**	I
	5		**NIEUERBRUG**	
(L. Grecht . . . *Connect Route 11)*	5		**WOERDEN.** A charming town with many historic buildings, a castle and a museum in the 16thC former Town Hall. There is a Cheese Market every Wednesday morning.	
	7	1	**HARMELEN**	
	5		**DE MEERN**	
LEFT, INTO *AMSTERDAM-RIJN* *KANAAL*	3	1		

		Map
Kms Locks	**Route 20**	*ref*

RIGHT, INTO 2
MERWEDE KANAAL

MERWEDE KANAAL   **UTRECHT.** A splendid town of high gabled   I
houses, picturesque water gates and winding canals,
once a Roman citadel, the fortress of the Franks,
the Seat of Ecclesiastical Sovereigns; now noted for
its trade fairs and particularly the twice yearly
industrial fair in March and September. Utrecht is
Holland's fourth largest city.
St. Agnes Convent, now the Central Museum, old
paintings, porcelain, 55ft Viking ship. St.
Catherine's Convent with museums of modern
ecclesiastical art, gold, silver and music machines;
Butchers' Guildhall 1673; Dom Cathedral, oldest
Gothic church in Holland with highest tower;
Railway Museum; Clock and Musical Boxes
Museum.

(Connect Routes 22, 23, 29)

Utrecht is a city of winding canals . . .

. . . once a Roman citadel, Utrecht is noted for its trade fairs.

Route 21 **Lemmer to Harlingen**

Distance   40kms
Number of locks   1
Minimum height above water   2m 40
Minimum depth of water   1m 70

Map
ref

PRINSES MARGRIET
KANAAL

LEMMER. A charming little harbour with shops   B
around and yachts alongside under the trees, in
fact, with your mast stepped, you have to watch
that your rigging does not become entangled with
the branches. It is a picture postcard setting and
popular as a result.
On the other side of the town is a shipyard around
which are industrial quays.
(Connect Route 35)

Lemmer.

	Kms	Locks	Route 21	Map ref
LEFT, LANGESLOOT	2			
RIGHT, EE OF BOOMSVAART	2			
(R. Woud sloot)	2			
		1	**SLOTEN.** An attractive little place, usually with many yachts lining its banks. It is said to be the smallest town in Friesland.	B
CROSS SLOTER MEER (R. Welle L. Woudsender Rakken)		5	**WOUDSEND**	
NAUWE WIJMERTS				
(L. Heegar Var R. Jelte Sloot . . . Connect Route 9)		3		
WIJDE WIJMERTS				
(R. to Sneek)		5	**IJLST**	
BOLSWARDERVAART		8	**BOLSWARD.** An old town that once belonged to the Hanseatic League; possesses a beautiful Town Hall, 16thC, one of the most impressive in Holland. St. Martinikerk, 1446 (painted ceilings, Baroque pulpit; Broerenkerk, 1270. (Connect Route 31)	A
ZEILVAART VAN HARLINGEN NAAR BOLSWARD (R. Trekvaart van Bolsward naar Leeuwarden . . . Connect Routes 13, 31)				
LEFT (str. on, Lathumer Vaart)		4		
		5	**ARUM**	
RIGHT (str. on, Bedelaarsvaart)		2		
		1	**KIMSWERD**	
		1	**HARLINGEN** (Connect Route 13)	

Route 22 **Lobith to Amsterdam**

Distance 120kms
Number of locks 2
Minimum height above water unlimited
Minimum depth of water 3m

	Kms	Locks		Map ref
GERMANY				
BOVEN RIJN			**LOBITH**	L
BIJLANDS KANAAL				
HOLLAND				
WAAL			**TOLKAMER**	
RIGHT FORK	4			
PANNERDENS KANAAL				
(L. Waal . . .				
Connect Route 25)				
LEFT FORK, RIJN	10			
(R. Ijssel . . .				
Connect Route 4)				
		3	**ARNHEM**	

19 **WAGENINGEN.** The town where the surrender documents were signed by Germany in 1945. Holland's most important agricultural university is here. An ancient town of great interest.

9 **RHENEN.** Advertised as a Pleasure Area but it is quite a pleasant place. There is an interesting zoo in which the animals appear to be completely free. Antique Chamber Museum; Gothic Church.

16 **WIJK BIJ DUURSTEDE.** One of the most K
important waterway junctions in Holland; an important port of the Middle Ages, where the River Rhine now becomes the River Lek.
A few miles away on the road to Utrecht is the village of Doorn, from 1920 to 1941 the home in

	Kms	Locks	Route 22	Map ref
RIJN			exile of the ex-Kaiser of Germany. Now a museum	K

RIJN

exile of the ex-Kaiser of Germany. Now a museum K
containing a large collection illustrating the history
of the German Royal House. Rusty horseshoes hang
over every door for good luck; photos, paintings and
statues of the late occupant are everywhere. In his
study there is a full size riding saddle (mounted on
a framework), on which he did all of his writing,
asserting that no man could be mentally alert unless
sitting absolutely erect

'GHT AT JUNCTION
INTO AMSTERDAM
RIJN KANAAL   1   2

(From L. Lek . . .   12
Connect Routes 23, 30)

(Junction Doorslag   1
Kanaal)

River Rijn at Rhenen.

				Map
	Kms	*Locks*	**Route 22**	*ref*
(L. Oudenrijn . . .	5		**UTRECHT**	I
Connect Route 20)			*(Connect Routes 20, 23, 29)*	
(Junction Kerkvaart	13		**BREUKELEN.** A beautiful and peaceful little	
to Loosedrecht Plassen)			town, a world away in all respects from Brooklyn,	
			New York to which it gave its name.	
	2		**OVER HOLLAND**	
(Junction Nive Wetering)				
(From R. Oude Vecht)	11			
(Junction L. Trekvaart	3		**WEESP**	
Gaasp. R. Small Weesp				
. . . Connect Routes 17, 29)				
(R. Muider Trekvaart	3			
. . . Connect Routes 17, 29				
(Connect Routes	8		**AMSTERDAM**	
6, 7, 11, 14, 15)				

Route 23 **Maasbracht to Utrecht**

Distance	150kms
Number of locks	19
Minimum height above water	4m
Minimum depth of water	2m 30

	Kms	*Locks*		*Map ref*
MAAS			**MAASBRACHT**	M
			(Connect Route 24)	
LEFT INTO KANAAL	3			
ESSEM-NEDERWEERT		1	**MILLERT**	*
(Junction, from L. Zuid-Willemsvaart—from Belgium. R. Noordervaart)				
ONTINUE AHEAD ON ZUID-WILLEMSVAART		1		
	1		**NEDERWEERT**	*
		1		
	4		**SOMEREN-EIND**	*
		2		
		1	**SOMEREN**	
(L. Eindhovens Broek Kanaal . . . Connect Route 1)	21			
		3		
		1	**HELMOND.** A pleasant little place in which is a 14thC Town Hall with a folklore museum.	*
		1		
		3	**AARLE-RIXTEL**	*
(L. Wilhelmina Kanaal . . . Connect Route 1)	3			
		1		
		2	**BEEK EN DONK**	*
		2		
	10		**VEGHEL**	*
		3		

* No Waterkaart.

| | | *Map* |
| Kms Locks | Route 23 | *ref* |

19   **s'HERTOGENBOSCH.** Capital of North Brabant   K
and a most interesting city with shopping area and
items of interest within walking distance. The
industry does not intrude. The statue in the market
square is of Hieronymous Bosch who was born here
in 1450. Magnificent Gothic cathedral with finest
example of Gothic architecture in Holland; Town
Hall 16thC; Museum, coins, weapons, maps, mss.

LEFT AT JUNCTION
(R. Dieze)
KANAAL ENGELEN-
HENRIETTEWAARD   I

LEFT INTO MAAS   6
(Connect Route 24)

s'Hertogenbosch has a magnificent Gothic cathedral.

	Kms	Locks	Route 23	Map ref
MAAS			**AMMERZODEN**	K
			HEUSDEN	
RIGHT INTO *HEUSDENS KANAAL*	9			
			AALBURG	
(R. Dode Arm)				
ANDELSE MAAS	6		**AALST**	
	6	I	**POEDEROIJENSEHOEK**	
MAAS				
	5		**WOUDRICHEM**	
LEFT IN BOVEN *MERWEDE* *(Connect Routes 5, 25)*				
	3		**GORINCHEM.** An old fortified town dating back to the 13thC, much fought over and still largely surrounded by 16thC walls and bastions.	
		I		
RIGHT, MERWEDE *KANAAL*				
	4		**ARKEL**	
RIGHT BEFORE LOCK			**MEERKERK**	
	12		**VIANEN.** An interesting town, an old rectangular fortress town with an attractive collection of mediaeval buildings including 15thC and 17thC gateways and a 15thC Town Hall.	
RIGHT IN LEK		I	**VREESWIJK**	I
LEFT INTO LEK *KANAAL*				
(From R. Amsterdam *Rijnkanaal)*	3			
from L. Doorslag Kanaal)	2	I		
RIGHT AT FORK	3			
			UTRECHT *(Connect Routes 20, 22, 29)*	

Route 24 Maastricht to Geertruidenberg

Distance	205kms
Number of locks	8
Minimum height above water	7m
Minimum depth of water	2m 20

	Kms	Locks		Map ref
JULIANAKANAAL			**MAASTRICHT.** Capital of Limburg, a pleasant town with shops and interest near the water, separated from the industrial part. There are churches, gateways, walls, bastions and many historic monuments in mediaeval Gothic, Renaissance and Baroque styles. Antiquities Museum; St. Servatius, earliest example of Gothic architecture in Europe; Church of St. John 14thC; Romanesque Basilica of Our Lady 11thC; St. Joseph's Church 1661.	M
(L. to join Zuid-Willemsvaart)				
(L. Maas)				
		1		
	12		**ELSLOO.** Pleasant little place with a 'Shipper's House' built in the Meuseland style of the 17thC; also a small church with valuable carvings.	
		1		
	8		**GREVENBICHT**	
	6		**ROOSTEREN**	
		1		
	9		**MAASBRACHT** *(Connect Route 23)*	
MAAS				
(From L. Kanaal Wessem-Nederweert)				
		1		
	9		**ROERMOND.** A most attractive town dominated by a beautiful Norman cathedral. Roermond is the seat of an R.C. Bishop. Gothic Munster Church 13thC; Folklore Museum.	
	6		**BUGGENUM**	

	Kms	Locks	Route 24	Map ref
MAAS	5		**HANSSUM**	M
	5		**KESSEL**	
	5	I	**BELFIELD**	
	9		**VENLO.** An industrial centre in beautiful surroundings. 14thC Town Hall with council room walled with Cordova leather.	
	12		**ARCEN**	
	12		**WANSSUM**	
	7		**VIERLINGSBEEK**	
	14	I	**GENNEP**	
	8		**CUYK**	
(From R. Mookerplas)	2		**MOOK.** There is a British War Cemetery here.	L
LEFT AT FORK *(R. Maas-Waalkanaal . . .* *Connect Route 25)*	3		**HEUMEN**	
	7	I	**GRAVE**	
	8		**RAVENSTEIN**	
	11		**MAASBOMMEL**	
(R. to Waal via Rossum) *lock . . . Connect Routes* *5, 23, 25)*	8	I	**LITH**	
(L. Kanaal Engelen- *Henriettewaard to* *s'Hertogenbosch . . .* *Connect Route 23)*	9		**HEDEL**	K
(R. Heusden's Kanaal joins *Boven Merwede, Waal)*	4		**AMMERZODEN**	
	6		**HEUSDEN.**	K
	6		**WAALWIJK**	
	14		**GEERTRUIDENBERG** *(Connect Routes 5, 10)*	

Route 25 Millingen a/d Rijn to Dordrecht

Distance	100kms
Number of locks	0
Minimum height above water	12m
Minimum depth of water	3m

		Kms *Locks*		*Map ref*

WAAL
(R. Pannerdens Kanaal
. . . Connect Route 22)

MILLINGEN a/d RIJN L

16 **NIJMEGEN.** An imperial city containing the ruins of the Valkhof, the court once occupied by Charlemagne; now a big, bustling city with splendid shops and shopping precinct but with trees and flowers as well. The River Waal flows wide and fast by the high quay walls and there is a lot of barge traffic.
St. Stephen's Church 13thC; Town Hall 16thC containing tapestries from the time of the Sun King; Weigh House 17thC.

(L. Maas-Waalkanaal to
Maas . . . Connect Route 24)

23 **OCHTEN**

3 **BENEDEN LEEUWEN**

(R. Amsterdam Rijn Kanaal
to Wijk bij Duurstede . . .
Connect Routes 22, 30)

River Waal near Nijmegen.

	Kms	Locks	Route 25	Map ref

WAAL — 5 — **TIEL.** Situated in the middle of what is known as orchard land; there is an annual fruit parade here on the second Saturday in September. Tiel is a former Hanseatic inland port with an interesting old quarter, ruined walls and a 16thC Guildhall furnished in Louis XIV and XV style.

(L. to Maas via Rossum lock . . . Connect Route 24) — 11

8 — **ZALTBOMMEL.** A charming small town. Gothic — K
St. Martin's Church; Maarten van Rossum House, collection of antiquities; Watergate, 15thC tower with carillon and mechanical horsemen.

(from L. Maas . . . Connect Route 24)

CONTINUE ON SAME WATERWAY, NOW BOVEN MERWEDE

21 — **GORINCHEM**

(R. Merwede Kanaal to Lek . . . Connect Routes 23, 30)

RIGHT FORK, BENEDEN MERWEDE (L. Nieuwe Merwede)

20 — **DORDRECHT**
(Connect Routes 11, 25)

Gorinchem.

Route 26 **Purmerend-Edam-Het Schouw**

PURMEREND to EDAM

Distance	10kms
Number of locks	0
Minimum height above water	unlimited
Minimum depth of water	1m 50

	Kms	Locks		Map ref
PURMER RINGVAART			**PURMEREND** *(Connect Routes 2, 6)*	G
	10		**EDAM.** A picture postcard little town that would be famous for its charm even if the red balls of cheeses did not come from here. Yachts line the quaint narrow streets, although few because Edam is small. Cheeses and souvenirs predominate as you would expect. Weigh House, collection of cheese-making appliances. Museum, with a 'floating' cellar.	

EDAM to HET SCHOUW

Distance	13 kms
Number of locks	1
Minimum height above water	3m 80
Minimum depth of water	1m 40

	Kms	Locks		Map ref
TREKVAART VAN MONNICKENDAM NAAR EDAM			**EDAM**	G
(R. Purmer Ringvaart)	2			
(R. Stinkevuil of Purmer Ee)		3	**LAGENDIJK**	
		1	**MONNICKENDAM.** You see the tower of the Grote Kerk as you approach, when you get near you hear the carillon striking the hour, nearer still you see the knights marching. It is a small town with a pretty harbour, shops and gabled houses around and many yachts. In the Stuttenburgh Inn, by the harbour, is a collection of mechanical musical instruments.	

	Kms	*Locks*	**Route 26**	

*CONTINUE AS
TREKVAART VAN
HET SCHOUW NAAR
MONNICKENDAM*

4   **BROEK IN WATERLAND**

3   **HET SCHOUW**

*JOIN NOORD
HOLLANDS KANAAL
(L. to Amsterdam)*   *(Connect Routes 2, 6)*

Route 27 **Stolpen to Medemblik**

Distance	29kms
Number of locks	5
Minimum height above water	3m 20
Minimum depth of water	2m 50

	Kms	Locks		Map ref
KANAAL STOLPEN-SCHAGEN			**STOLPEN** *(Connect Route 7)*	G
(Junction Groote Sloot)	2			
	2		**SCHAGEN.** A pretty little town, celebrated for the folklore pageant held during July and August.	
CONTINUE AS KANAAL SCHAGEN-KOLHORN		1		
	7		**KOLHORN**	
(R. Kanaal Alkmaar-Kolhorn to Alkmaar . . . Connect Route 3)				
(Junction L. Waard Kanaal R. Groetkanaal)	2			
		1		
RIGHT AT JUNCTION (L. Sloot vaart . . . Connect Route 8)	6			
			MIDDENMEER	
	10	3	**MEDEMBLIK** *(Connect Route 8)*	
IJSSELMEER				

Route 28 Ter Apel to Groningen

Distance	50kms
Number of locks	6
Minimum height above water	unlimited
Minimum depth of water	2m

	Kms	Locks		Map ref
TER APELKANAAL			**TER APEL**	*
		1		
	10		**MUSSELKANAAL**	
MUSSEL KANAAL		3		
	9		**STADSKANAAL**	
STADS KANAAL		2		
RIGHT, PEKELER HOOFDIEP	3			
		4		
	12		**OUDE PEKELA**	
RIGHT, WINSCHOTERZIJL				
	7		**WINSCHOTEN**	
		1		
	9		**NIEUWESCHANS**	
WESTER WOLD SE IJMEERER SIELTIEF				
		1		
	6		**NIEUWE STATENZIJL**	
DOLLARD				
STADS KANAAL	5		**BAREVELD**	
(R. to Winschoterdiep via Veendam) *GREVELINGSKANAAL*	14		**HOOGEZAND**	
LEFT INTO WINSCHOTERDIEP				
	9		**GRONINGEN**	

* No Waterkaart.

Route 29 Utrecht to Muiden

Distance	38kms
Number of locks	2
Minimum height above water	4m
Minimum depth of water	2m 25

	Kms	Locks		Map ref
VECHT			**UTRECHT**	I
			(Connect Routes 20, 22, 23)	
	4		**OUD-ZUILEN**	
		I		
	4		**MAARSSEN.** A beautiful village and surroundings, with 18thC waterside houses.	
VECHT *(R. to Loosdrechtse Plassen)*	3			
(L. to Amsterdam-Rijn Kanaal)	2		**BREUKELEN** *(Connect Route 22)*	
(L. to Amsterdam-Rijn Kanaal and Angstel)	3			
(R. to Loosdrechtse Plassen)	I			
		I	**LOENEN.** A pretty village in wooded surroundings. Castle Ter Horst 1557.	
VECHT	2		**VREELAND.** You can see unusual wood carvings and basketware made here.	I
(R. to Hilversum)	2		**HET HEMELTJE**	
RIGHT *(str. on lock into Amsterdam-Rijn Kanaal)*	5			
	3		**HINDERAM**	
(R. Trekvaart naar Karnemelk Sloot)	2			

Leonen is in wooded surroundings.

Kms	Locks	Route 29	Map ref
3		**WEESP**	

RIGHT
(L. to Amsterdam-Rijn Kanaal)

	I		
3		**MUIDEN.**	

(L. Muider Trekvaart to
Amsterdam-Rijn Kanaal
R. Naarder Trekvaart to
Naarden)   *(Connect Route 17)*

Route 30 Wijk Bij Duurstede to Krimpen Aan De Lek

Distance	61kms
Number of locks	1
Minimum height above water	14m
Minimum depth of water	2m 70

	Kms	Locks		Map ref
NEDER RIJN ACROSS AMSTERDAM-RIJN KANAAL AT JUNCTION TO LEK			**WIJK BIJ DUURSTEDE**	K
	2		**RAVENSWAAIJ**	
	10		**CULEMBORG.** There are many gabled houses in this old free city of Gelderland, also ruined fortress walls and gates. Late Gothic Town Hall; Church of St. Barbara 14thC.	
		1		

River Lek at Vianen.

	Kms	Locks	Route 30

(R. Lekkanaal . . .   10   **VIANEN**
Connect Route 23)
(R. Merwedekanaal)
(L. Merwedekanaal to
   Boven Merwede . . .
Connect Routes 5, 23, 25)

           1   **VREESWIJK**

          20   **SCHOONHOVEN.** An extremely pretty village, a silver centre; visitors are welcome at the many small workshops to watch silver filigree jewellery being made. There is a Silversmiths' Museum, an historic Weigh House and gin store house. Gothic Town Hall dates from 1452.

          18   **KRIMPEN AAN DE LEK**
JOIN NIEUWE MAAS   *(Connect Route 11)*
(L. Noord to Beneden
Merwede and Oude Maas . . .
Connect Routes 11, 12, 25)

Route 31 **Workum to Leeuwarden**

Distance   37kms
Number of locks   0
Minimum height above water   2m 50
Minimum depth of water   1m 50

	Kms	Locks		Map ref
TREKVAART VAN WORKUM NAAR BOLSWARD			**WORKUM**	A
(L. Van Panhuijs Kanaal to Makkum)	7			
(L. Makkumer Vaart to Makkum)	4		**BOLSWARD** *(Connect Route 21)*	
TREKVAART VAN BOLSWARD NAAR LEEUWARDEN				
	3		**BURGWERD**	
	4		**WOMMELS**	
(Junction with Franeker Vaart—L. Franeker . . . Connect Route 13. R. Sneek Connect Route 33)	6			
	1		**BAARD**	
RIGHT INTO VAN HARINXMA KANAAL	5			
	7		**LEEUWARDEN** *(Connect Route 13)*	

Route 32 **Zutphen to Hoogersmilde**

Distance   125kms
Number of locks   7
Minimum height above water   6m
Minimum depth of water   1m 80

	Kms	Locks		Map ref
			ZUTPHEN	*
			(Connect Route 4)	
TWENTHE KANAAL	3			
		1		
	17		**LOCHEM.** A popular summer resort in a setting of oak forests. Town Hall 1640.	
		13	**GOOR**	
LEFT TWENTHE KANAAL *(str. on Twenthe Kanaal to Enschede)*				
		1		
	21		**ALMELO.** A weaving town in an important textile manufacturing area. Although an industrial town it is old with many attractions.	
LEFT, OVERIJSSELS KANAAL				
	4		**VRIEZENVEEN**	
(L. to Zwolle . . .	15		**VROOMSHOP**	
Connect Routes 4, 34)	8		**HARDENBERG**	
	2		**GRAMSBERGEN.** A charming town with a great deal of historic interest.	
		1		
COEVORDEN- VECHTKANAAL				
		1		
	7		**COEVORDEN.** In the middle of an oil producing region but there is not the hideous industrial spoilation that you would expect. Many hundreds of small wells have been drilled and you see little spurts of flame amongst trees and farms and buildings and you smell the oily smell.	

* No Waterkaart.

			Map
Kms	*Locks*	**Route 32**	*ref*

KANAAL COEVORDEN-			*
ZWINDEREN			
	2		
	2	**ZWINDEREN**	
LEFT, HOOGEVEENSE			
VAART			
(Connect Route 18)			
RIGHT, LINTHORST-			
HOMANKANAAL	8		
	1		
	16	**BEILEN**	
BEILER VAART			
BRUNSTINGER			
	9	**HOOGERSMILDE**	
		(Connect Route 19)	
DRENTSCHE			
HOOFDVAART			

* There is no Waterkaart for this route.

Route 33 Zwartsluis to Sneek

Distance   71kms
Number of locks   2
Minimum height above water   2m 95
Minimum depth of water   1m 25

			Map
	Kms	*Locks*	*ref*
MEPPELER DIEP			**ZWARTSLUIS.** Barges congregate here, three and four deep under the trees in a pretty setting and often crowding the lift bridge at the end of the Meppeler Diep; but you can go round by Zwarte Water where you will see the yacht haven. There are all shops here and it is a very pleasant little place.	C

		1
LEFT, BEUKERS	3	
GRACHT		
(R. Meppeler Diep to		
Meppel . . .		
Connect Routes 18, 34)		

ck to
ukers Gracht.

			Map
	Kms	*Locks*	**Route 33**	*ref*

ACROSS BELTER
WIJDE

7 **GIET HORN.** You will be in your element here— C
literally— for there are no roads and all movement
is by water. Practically every house is an island and
everything moves around by boat. It is a very
pretty village with quaint houses and bridges and a
church (with a nautical congregation of course).

(L. Thijssengracht) 2

KANAAL BEUKERS-
STEENWIJK

5 **STEENWIJK.** A former fortress town with some
remaining bastions. St. Clements Church 15thC.

KANAAL OSSENZIJL-
STEENWIJK

(L. Steenwijker diep) 1

13 **OSSENZIJL**
RIGHT, LINDE

1

LEFT, JONKERS OF 3
HELOMA VAART
(str. on Linde)

	Kms	*Locks*	**Route 33**	*Map ref*
LEFT, TJONGER (*Connect Route 19*)			**ZEVENBUURT**	
RIGHT, PIER CHRISTIAANSLOOT	7			
		2	**ECHTENERBRUG**	
TJEUKEMEER	1			B
FOLLEGA SLOOT		5	**FOLLEGA**	
RIGHT, GROTE BREKKEN INTO PRINSES MARGRIET KANAAL	3			
ACROSS KOEVORDE	8			
PRINSES MARGRIET KANAAL				B
RIGHT FORK WESTERBRUGSLOOT	3			
LEFT, HOUKESLOOT (*str. on Sneeker Meer*)	4			
		4	**SNEEK.** Described as a yachting paradise. From the beautiful little harbour a channel leads out into Sneekermeer and there is a great deal of movement afloat, and later ashore with the usual 'sailing crowd' conviviality. Silver souvenirs are made here for sale all over Holland. Frisian Shipping Museum; Town Hall in Frisian Rococo; Picturesque Watergate with defence towers 1613.	
(*Connect Route 13*)				

Route 34   Zwolle to Groningen

Distance	98kms
Number of locks	5
Minimum height above water	8m
Minimum depth of water	1m 55

* There is no Waterkaart for this route.

Route 35 Zwartsluis to Lemmer

Distance	41kms
Number of locks	3
Minimum height above water	unlimited
Minimum depth of water	2m 25

	Kms	Locks		Map ref
ZWOLSE DIEP			**ZWARTSLUIS**	C
			(Connect Route 34)	
	3		**GENEMUIDEN.** The centre of an unusual matting industry. The Achterweg here is the only street in Holland in which smoking is not allowed.	
(L. Zwarte Meer to Ketelhaven . . . Connect Route 17)	3			
ZWANEDIEP				
		1		
LEFT INTO	6			
ZWOLSE VAART		1		
	7	1	**MARKNESSE**	
	6		**EMMELOORD.** In the centre of the Noordoost-polder, all straight canals and straight roads, all comparatively new because it was all beneath the sea thirty years ago. From the polder tower you can see the wide expanse of reclaimed land.	

— —

	Kms	Locks		
EURK RVAART			**EMMELOORD**	
	6		**TOLLEBEEK**	
	6		**URK.** A former island and now part of the Noordoostpolder. A fishing port with hefty fishing boats bustling everywhere—yachts take second place. It is not a place in which to stay longer than necessary; the requirements of the fish auction take precedence over all other activities here. There are all shops in the quaint little town and some inhabitants still wear traditional costume. Be	

Kms	Locks		*Map ref*
		Route 35	

careful about photographing them on a Sunday,   C
however, for these devout Protestant townsfolk may
sometimes object.

IJSSELMEER   I

— —

LEMSTER VAART   **EMMELOORD**

     16   I   **LEMMER**
                 (Connect Route 21)

IJSSELMEER

Traditional dress and
fishing boats at Urk.

From Belgium into Holland

Route BH/1 Liege to Maastricht

Distance	28kms
Number of locks	1
Minimum height above water	4m 50
Minimum depth of water	2m 50

	Kms	Locks	
			LIEGE
RIVER MEUSE merges			
with CANAL ALBERT	1		**KING ALBERT STATUE** on Ile de Monsin marking the start of the Canal Albert.
	1		**HERSTAL**
	3		**VIVEGNIS**
(R. Canal de Haccourt	5		**HACCOURT**
a Vise)			
			RIVER MEUSE/MAAS running parallel on RIGHT is FRONTIER for 63 kilometres
JOIN FROM LEFT	4		**LIXHE**
CANAL ALBERT	3		
CANAL TERNAAIEN	4	1	**PETIT LANAYE**
			FRONTIER
MAAS	7		**MAASTRICHT**
			(Connect Route 24)

Route BH/2 **Neerharen to Maastricht**

Distance	6kms
Number of locks	2
Minimum height above water	4m 50
Minimum depth of water	2m 10

ZUID-WILLEMSVAART   **NEERHAREN**

FRONTIER

3   **SMEERMAS**

2

3   **MAASTRICHT**
(*Connect Route 24*)

Maastricht is close to the Belgian frontier.

Route BH/3 **Losen to Nederweert**

Distance   12kms
Number of locks   1
Minimum height above water   4m
Minimum depth of water   2m 50

ZUID-WILLEMSVAART   **LOSEN**

            3   **FRONTIER**
              1
            7   **WEERT**

         LEFT   2
    (from R. Kanaal
Wessem-Nederweert)   **NEDERWEERT**
                  (Connect Route 23)

Route BH/4 Ghent to Terneuzen

Distance	36kms
Number of locks	1
Minimum height above water	unlimited
Minimum depth of water	5m 50

	Kms	Locks	
CANAL DE GHENT			GHENT
A TERNEUZEN			
	5		LANGERBRUGGE
	4		BAC
(R. Canal de Moervaart)			
	1		TERDONK
	8		ZELZATE
			FRONTIER
	2		SAS-VAN-GHENT
	8		SLUISKIL
	8	1	TERNEUZEN

5   So many Waterways

Cruising along between the river banks you see away over there the masts of yachts sprouting from the grass, and rounding a corner you pass a small harbour cut into the bank or a group of yachts nodding at their moorings upon a lake.

Over to your left or right across a field you see a flag fluttering and pick out the wheelhouse, the bent-back foremast of a barge; presently the unmistakable donk-donk-donk of the deep voiced engine comes floating over the meadow.

Seeing so much around you and so far away brings home to you the realisation that this land really is flat, and that much of Holland is flat because much of Holland is man-made.

From an inland cruising point of view the flatness of the country is ideal. In my book on the French canals I have covered the waterways of that country in twenty-five Cruise Routes in which the number of locks totals 1,455. In this book I have covered Holland in thirty-five Cruise Routes in which there are 118 locks.

I happen to have an odd, warm regard for locks as friendly focal points of waterway life (an opinion not necessarily shared by my dear ladder-swarming foredeckhand), but I do accept that too many locks can limit a worthwhile cruising programme when time is limited, as it usually is.

The Cruise Routes in this book have not been designed with any idea of lock avoidance but they happen to have worked out as follows:—

Number of Cruise Routes with					0 locks	.....	8
,,	,,	,,	,,	,,	1 ,,	.....	7
,,	,,	,,	,,	,,	2 ,,	.....	5
,,	,,	,,	,,	,,	3 ,,	.....	3
,,	,,	,,	,,	,,	4 ,,	.....	1
,,	,,	,,	,,	,,	5 ,,	.....	3

,,	,,	,,	,,	,,	6	,,	· · · · · 1
,,	,,	,,	,,	,,	7	,,	· · · · · 3
,,	,,	,,	,,	,,	8	,,	· · · · · 2
,,	,,	,,	,,	,,	12	,,	· · · · · 1
,,	,,	,,	,,	,,	19	,,	· · · · · 1

Not only can you cruise greater distances with less effort in the Dutch waterways, you have a much greater variety of stopping places, for in the canals you can stop anywhere alongside the banks (but not near to locks or bridges), or in harbours or yacht stations. On the lakes you are likely to find the landing stages of yacht stations most convenient but you can tie up anywhere alongside banks and islands so long as you avoid the front gardens of private houses and do not moor where you see a notice '*Verboden Toegang*'. On the big rivers a bank-side, pontoon or quay mooring would be uncomfortable, to say the least, so that harbours, yacht stations or the dredged lakes adjoining the rivers should be sought.

There is a big choice of yacht stations or harbours, small and enormous. In private and municipal marinas the charge is calculated on L.O.A. There will always be such a harbour or station nearby.

Almost every town and village in Holland seems to be situated on a river, lake or canal, so conveniently situated indeed that in a number of places you see lines and lines of modern, attractive, box-shaped houseboats contributing to a solution of the housing problem.

In fact there are so many waterways that no book of manageable size could attempt to include all of the smaller ones. In the first half of this book are shown thirty-five suggested Cruise Routes, waterways covering Holland from one terminal point to another so that the reader can link up from one to another in conjunction with the Cruise Route map shown on page 8 to plan the exploration of any area of interest. Every major town, waterway and lake is included.

There are sometimes alternatives and even alternatives to the alternatives, making an embarrassing choice of waterway riches. But these smaller alternatives are all clearly shown on the superb water maps published annually by the Dutch Government. Many of the smaller canals have ceased to be navigable except by small craft and some do not allow craft with engines; on others, and in some lakes, permits are necessary. There are no restrictions on the Cruise Routes in this book.

Since you can stop anywhere no specific stopping places are indicated (the very, very few places where berthing is not allowed are not of interest as stopping places anyway). There are thousands of miles of canal banks, yacht havens, yacht stations, yacht marinas, yacht clubs and you can take it for granted that you will be made welcome everywhere. The Dutch are friendly, sympathetic towards yachting (there is one boat for every 200 inhabitants in Holland), well disposed towards visiting yachtsmen and the British flag in particular, almost invariably English speaking and helpful. In established yachting harbours you obviously have to pay for the facilities offered, showers, bars etc., whereas if you tie up to quay or bank there is no charge. Yacht clubs are inclined to offer initial free moorings if you are a yacht club member in your own country but there is not always room, particularly in the height of the season.

Another unusual feature about Holland is that you can go from one end of the country to another with a fixed mast. To make a comparison with France once more, you can get no further up the Seine than Rouen without unstepping your mast; in Holland you can keep your mast up from Flushing to the Amstel Yacht Harbour, from the Hook of Holland to Amsterdam, from Ijmuiden to Amsterdam, from Den Helder to Amsterdam, from Delfzijl to Amsterdam. It must be admitted that the store of patience that you accumulate through lock-free cruising is dissipated as you wait for bridges to open. Much of the time they open for you quickly and efficiently, particularly if you are not in a hurry. When time presses you assuredly come up against bridges that remain closed to you during rush hour periods ashore and should you have a really urgent need to make progress that will undoubtedly be on a Saturday morning when you are stuck between two bridges that do not open until Monday morning.

A small chart of waterways without fixed bridges (*Vaarwegen Zonder Vaste Bruggen*), is issued free by the ANWB but the descriptions of opening/closing times shown upon it are written in Dutch. These notes provide a hint of frustrations to be anticipated by the fixed-mast yachtsman, pointing out that the railway bridge in Amsterdam, on the route in from Aalsmeer, opens only at night; that the road bridge at Sassenheim, between Leiden and Haarlem, opens once a day; that bridges on the Oude Rijn, before Muiden on the way to the Ijsselmeer and from Ketelmeer, are only opened two or three times a day; that long delays should be expected in the Ooster Scheldt, Hollands Diep, either side of the Nieuwe Waterweg at Rotterdam, west of Gouda and south of Haarlem; limited headroom, (10m), between Blokzijl and the Ketelmeer up to 1st May and after 16th October; that the bridge on the Van Starkenborgh Kanaal, before Groningen, is closed on Saturdays;

and, finally, that some bridges need twenty-four hours notice if required to open on a Saturday.

Advance planning may be possible to avoid such delays, however, because the opening times of all bridges and locks is shown in Part 11 of the Almanak voor Watertoerisme, of which more later. It should also be stressed that these delays would only be experienced by yachts with fixed masts.

With your mast up you will obviously want to sail. You will see Dutch yachts doing so but in my experience it is a hair-raising occupation. On the big waterways you have streams of urgent ships, barges, passenger steamers, tugs and their tows, ferries, to all of which you must defer. The wind is never in the right quarter and to want to go about with a Rijn-Dusseldorfer churning close behind your transom is about as enjoyable an experience for me as would be a cycle ride on a Grand Prix circuit. Yet I must admit that Dutch yachtsmen do it with great panache, dodging in and out of groynes, cheerful, laughing, nonchalant.

On the big waterways you have streams of urgent ships, barges, passenger steamers, tugs and their tows, ferries and all.

On smaller waterways the proximity of the banks seems to give you such a terrifying illusion of speed that you appear to be hurtling through the meadows. Even now I shudder to recall such an incident when we were flashing along, encountering vast barges that left us the narrowest of gaps just when the wind gusted strongest, seeing a bridge ahead, unable to leave the helm yet wanting the main off, hearing the foredeckhand below accompanying the too loud radio in a happy song and impervious to my cries. The moral of this sad story, if you are determined to sail, is to have your anchor ready to let go at all times.

We are always glad to return to Holland because it is such a bright, welcoming place, polished clean as though for our benefit, the people trained to speak our language as though for the pleasure of greeting us. In no other country are facilities so good for the cruising yachtsman, in no other country are the delights of town and village so conveniently situated by the water, not behind forbidding warehouse walls and grim gates like a poor relation, but accepted as a part of everyday life; even waterside industry gives the impression of being as clean as it can be. Holland has the richest cruising ground of any country in terms of variety, with inland seas, rivers, seemingly endless miles of canals and a lake almost around every corner.

Cruising through Holland is a delight and navigation on most of the Dutch waterways is simple, even for beginners, BUT two obvious points need to be stressed. You have to get there and, once there, you should choose your waterways according to your experience.

To take the second point first. If you have any thought of idyllic drifting through the major waterway sections, singing the Eton boating song and exchanging pleasantries with pipe smoking, clog wearing, baggy panted bargees you are in for a shock. The major waterway sections are rough and tough, completely lacking in sympathy for the inexperienced small boat skipper. After a warning of this nature you will be pleased to learn that there are many, many mooring places just off the big rivers, numerous yacht harbours and berths, such as the yacht harbours at Drimmelen, Lage Zwaluwe, Moerdijk, Willemstad and Gorinchem. In seeking to avoid the busiest waterways it is no solution to consult the International Classification of Waterways, referred to later, as a guide. The Waal and the Noord Hollandsch, for instance, are both Class V waterways; the Waal is hair-raising whilst a small boy in a rowing boat can relieve the monotony of the long, wide, vacant stretches of the Noord-Hollandsch.

Next is the problem of how to get to Holland. Those yachtsmen who do not see this as a problem will, I hope, bear with me when I explain that many readers of my previous books have had little or no experience of navigation or seamanship. Quite a lot of the long distance cruising folk we have met in the European waterways and Mediterranean have had no previous experience at all, in fact it now seems to us that the less experience you have the more likely you are to go.

Most boat owners have ambitions to cruise beyond the range of their experience and most would do so if not restricted by time. Many seize the opportunity on retirement and the majority of long distance crews are composed of man and wife, usually retired, often inexperienced, who manage splendidly in the waterways and in Mediterranean harbour-hopping; if they will allow me to address them like a Dutch uncle I will advise that they should not attempt the open sea passage to Holland because there are too many hazards and too much traffic. They can easily reach the Dutch waterways through France and/or Belgium.

Many cruises start from the Solent area and most seem to prefer to make for Le Havre; consideration should be given to crossing from further east to Calais, Dunkerque, Nieuwport or Ostend. From each of these harbours you can cruise inland to Holland in a quarter of the time that it would take from Le Havre.

But if time is of no account and the route from the Seine is preferred, you should turn into the Oise at Conflans and up into Belgium, along the Charleroi-Brussels canal, (which will take you down the exciting Sloping Lock of Ronquières), across to the Zuid-Willemsvaart and into Holland that way.

All routes from France are described in my book, *Through the French Canals* (Nautical Books) and routes from Belgium are described in later pages.

Having reached the inland waterways of France or Belgium the 'back way' into Holland, mentioned above, is suggested for the inexperienced in preference to crossing the Wester-Scheldt. This waterway is as wide as a sea, the port of Antwerp is no place in which to cut your cruising teeth and the other 'exit', the Ghent-Terneuzen Canal I have described as Belgium's back yard. In fact this Dutch strip 'stuck on' to Belgium and separated from the main part of Holland by the Wester-Scheldt is of no interest to the inland cruising man. The Ghent-Terneuzen Canal leads into Belgium, as does the Scheldt up to Antwerp, and are therefore described in the second part of the book.

With sufficient sea-going experience the easiest and quickest way into Holland is through Flushing (Vlissengen), from where Cruise Route number 11 (the Cruise Routes in Holland are set out in the second half of the book), guides you into Holland.

Continuing up the Dutch coast, the next way in is through the lock at Stellendam into the Haringvliet to connect with Route 12.

You can sail straight into the Nieuwe Waterweg at the Hook of Holland and Route 14 will direct you up towards Rotterdam and fairly quickly out of it on the Delfshaven se Schie, although the second 'turning' to port after this would take you into the premier yacht club of Holland. (One reason for the tremendous volume of shipping at Rotterdam, by the way, is the small tidal range, under 2m at springs, so that ships can come in here at any time.)

Locking in at Ijmuiden is the next entry into Holland. Approaching the locks you should take the waterway to the south of the island to the smallest lock unless you are signalled to share a larger lock. Route 15 will take you to Amsterdam, connecting with five other routes. If you find the Noordzeekanaal too commercial you can turn off to the right into Zijkanaal C on Route 16.

The next entry above Ijmuiden is at Den Helder, the principal naval base of Holland, in fact apart from the fishing boats Den Helder is run by the Royal Netherlands Navy. There is limited mooring accommodation for visiting yachts except during the Annual Regatta that takes place in early July. Den Helder connects with Routes 7 and 8. Veerhaven, opposite Den Helder, is a ferry terminal and must not be entered.

In to the Wadden Zee and across to starboard you see the long grey sentinel of the Afsluitdijk standing guard with the locks at either end, Den Oever and Kornwerder Zand, leading into the Ijsselmeer.

Across the Wadden Zee from Den Helder is Harlingen, from where the Van Harinxa Kanaal leads in to Friesland connecting with Routes 13 and 21. It must have been some time before my first visit to Holland that I read *The Riddle of the Sands* and, in following the adventures amongst the dunes, I had a hazy impression of it all happening up in the north somewhere. Many people are surprised to learn that the islands ringing the Wadden Zee are 'lower down', in terms of latitude, than Grimsby.

Further on around the north coast of Holland you could lock into the Lauwers Zee and join up with Routes 9 and 13.

From here it is a short sail round the corner and into the Eems, with the German coastline away over to port and the unattractive harbour of Delfzijl to starboard, leading to Route 9.

Further on into the Dollard the last entry from the sea into

In through the lock at Stellendam.

Holland is at Nieuwe Statenzijl, on the Wester Wold and also on the German border.

The Dutch coast ends and the German coast begins; at Emden the Dortmund-Ems Kanaal leads away into further inland waterway exploration.

The connecting routes from Germany into Holland and from Belgium into Holland are listed at the end of the Cruise Routes Section.

Holland is a small country, 120 miles from east to west and 190 miles from north to south and about 20% of that land has been reclaimed from the sea, an ideal cruising ground because it accepts so completely the waterway life, making provision for waterway needs with adjacent fuel and shops, bottled gas, boat harbours everywhere. There is a great deal of interest concentrated in the south where you are never far from a place name that you recognise. In the north there are the wide open spaces for those who prefer them, in Friesland and Groningen and Drenthe where the country is flat agricultural land and towns are few and far between.

With 13 million people in its 14 million square miles Holland has the highest population density in the world, the greatest numbers living in the south because more industry, larger towns and opportunities are there. More than half live below sea level.

6 Planning the Dutch Cruise

No formalities are required to take your boat into Holland and therefore there is no need to seek 'planning permission' for the cruise you select. If you happen to be a member of a yacht club you could carry your membership card but we have never been asked for evidence of this nature. The only frontier documents required are valid passports for each person onboard. Ship's stores that are clearly intended for use onboard may be freely imported. You must report your arrival to the nearest Customs harbour office. You must also report on leaving Holland.

High speed motor boats must be registered in advance with the Royal Netherlands Motor Boat Club, Koninginneweg 51, Amsterdam. The 'master' of a fast motor boat must be at least 18 years of age; the helmsman of a sailing or motor boat must be at least 16 on the canals and 17 on the rivers.

The planning necessary for your Dutch cruise is mainly concerned with deciding where you want to go and then getting the necessary charts and rules.

I explain in the next chapter that navigation is mainly a matter of keeping out of the way but on the big rivers you are supposed ('required' would be a better word, particularly if your boat is over 15 tons) to have onboard the appropriate Rules.

There are separate Rules for the Rijn (Rhine), known by the simple name of *Rijnvaartpolitiereglement*; whilst you are trying to pronounce this I should mention that the Rijn is not known by this name where it flows through Holland, nor even by one alternative name, so that Rijn Rules apply on the Waal, Lek, Merwede etc.

The four Great Rivers that flow across Holland would certainly be more easily identifiable if they kept to the names they started with (although one cannot complain about the change from Meuse to Maas which at least sounds similar), but it is not a question of the continuation of the same waterway for the Rijn, after crossing the German frontier, splits up into three, the Waal, the Neder-Rijn and the Geldersche Ijssel. The river that starts off as the Neder-Rijn changes its name to the Lek. The river that starts off as the Waal changes its name three times to the Boven Merwede, the Beneden Merwede and Noord. The Ijssel branches off north on its own to the Ijsselmeer leaving the others with the burden of river traffic and to join up together again near Rotterdam. On these rivers the Rijn Rules apply (and also on the small part of the Ems adjacent to Dutch territory up in the north). Therefore if your planning includes cruising on any of these rivers, as it is almost bound to, you should send for a copy of the *Rijnvaartpolitiereglement*.

You should also have onboard a copy of the *Algemeen Reglement Van Politie Voor Rivieren* (General Police Rules for Rivers and Canals), and a copy of the *Vaarglement* (Rules to prevent collisions etc.). This latter set of rules has been translated into English in the *West European Pilot* (including also regulations for the Wester Scheldt). The *Algemeen Reglement Van Politie Voor Rivieren* and the *Vaareglement* are reproduced in Part 1 (Deel 1), of the Almanak voor Watertoerisme which you must have.

Part 11 of the Almanak gives tide tables, opening times of bridges and locks, particulars of towns and harbours and is published annually in the spring. Both parts are written in Dutch but much of the contents can be understood.

But first of all you will want to plan your cruise of Holland and when you have decided upon the areas you would like to visit, the index to the Cruise Routes and the Cruise Route Map will show you which routes are appropriate.

Zeeland and south west Holland are fine for sailing; in the estuaries that still have tidal access to the sea the ebb and flow are strong with a tidal range from 2m to $3\frac{1}{2}$m. In the estuary sailing here you can expect almost the same conditions as at sea and if your prefer cruising through towns and villages along narrower waterways this is not the area for you.

You will pass through Zeeland on Cruise Route 11 and visit the 'recommended-to-see' towns of Middelburg, Veere and Willemstad. You are obviously most likely to explore Zeeland if you enter Holland at Flushing. Whilst on the subject of Cruise Route 11, if you wish to avoid the possibility of delay at the bridges in Dordrecht (and if your mast height will clear 8m), you can turn left when you come out into Hollands Diep by Willemstad; through the Haringvliet to turn right into the Spui and so join Route 12, then through

Rotterdam along the Nieuwe Maas, turning left into the Hollands Ijssel.

Across from Zeeland the next adjacent lowest part of the country is what is known as the Big, or Great, Rivers Area and you may well enter Holland at the bottom right hand corner of this area (from Belgium), to join Cruise Routes 23 and 24. It is not possible to plan any route up into Holland without some contact with the big rivers since they span the country. You may find them exciting, of course, and they are certainly full of interest but all of the big rivers all of the time demand your constant vigilance to cope with the shipping and the currents. Do not assume that because you sail in Southampton Water or the Thames that you know all about busy waterways; to compare commercial traffic in Southampton Water with that in the Nieuwe Maas is like comparing the traffic in Chipping Sodbury High Street with that in Piccadilly.

Typical waterside—Haarlem.

The Neder-Rijn is a less busy cross-country waterway and it is also more beautiful. Cruise Routes 22 and 30 refer.

Looking north from the big river belt across Holland, the left hand or western side sparkles with attractive towns, lakes, sports centres—all the 'happenings' are in this area because it possesses the greatest concentration of population.

The way in to this area from the sea is along the busy Noordzeekanaal from Ijmuiden (Route 14). The Hook of Holland is further south. From the southernmost way in, Route 11 from Flushing leads to Amsterdam. From the inland waterways of Belgium, Route 23 leads up to Utrecht; from the inland waterways of Germany, Route 22 takes you to Amsterdam.

Whichever way you plan to come in to Holland, no waterway cruise of the country would be complete without a visit to the attractive area of Utrecht and Zuid-Holland and including that part of Noord-Holland up to, say, Alkmaar. The bordering Ijsselmeer entails a different consideration of sailing and harbour considerations.

Above Alkmaar the waterways are not so interesting and seem to 'go on a bit' if you understand what I mean. My personal signal for recognising that a waterway has gone on for too long, too straight or too far without interest is that it seems to start going uphill or downhill; the illusion is quite strong when I have been staring straight ahead for hour after hour and the engine conspires to support this illusion, seeming to struggle when I am going uphill as though imploring me to change down into a non-existent third gear and running away free on my downhill illusions. At such times the foredeckhand appears frequently from below to enquire if we have Got To Anything Interesting Yet. Needless to say, when fairy-tale castles, fairy-tale villages, historic bridges come into view, on other occasions, I shout in vain for her attention.

Up through Noord-Holland and you reach Den Helder (a connection also on Routes 7 and 8), beyond which lies the opportunity of deep-sea sailing in the Wadden Zee. If you are sufficiently experienced and adventurous you can sail to the islands of Texel, Vlieland and Terschelling.

On the other side of the Ijsselmeer are the canals and lakes of Friesland, Groningen and Drenthe with old Zuyder Zee towns, Harlingen on the Wadden Zee and a great deal of yachting activity throughout the area which is covered by a number of connecting Cruise Routes. The town of Groningen is attractive but the province is not. Every country is attractive and dull in parts and

the dull part of Holland has been pushed away up into this north
east corner.

When you have planned your cruise you can make your
selection of publications from the following list:—

List of Publications

West European Pilot
obtainable from L. J. Harri, BV Prins Hendrikkade 94/95, 1012 AE
   Amsterdam.
Almanak Voor Watertoerisme, Vol. I*
                          Vol. II
(*this contains the Algemeen Reglement van Politie and the
Vaarreglement)
Rijnvaartpolitiereglement
Charts of the waterways (waterkaarts), cover the country with the
exception of Noord-Holland, Drenthe, Twenthe-Salland-Achterhoek
and the bottom part of Noord-Brabant.
Map references (the letters), in the Route Details Section refer to the
following:—

A	Midden-Friesland Groningen and North Friesland
B	Zuidwest-Friesland Frisian Lakes
C	Noordwest-Overijssel
D	Gelderse Ijssel
E	Randmeren
F	Alkmaar-Den Helder
G	Amsterdam-Alkmaar (Alkmaar-Den Helder)
H	Hollandse Plassen
I	Vechtplassen
J	Grote Rivieren Westblad
K	Grote Rivieren Middenblad
L	Grote Rivieren Oostblad
M	Limburgse Maas
N	Biesbos
O	Veerse Meer
P	Vinkeveense Plassen
R	Loosdrechtse Plassen
S	Grevelingenmeer

When ordering the full title, above, should be stated.

Ordinary tourist maps (toeristenkaarts), are available for the whole of the country and are useful in planning visits to places (by hired bicycle?), away from the waterways.

1	Noord-Holland
2	Friesland
3	Groningen
4	Drenthe
5	Zuid-Holland
6	Utrecht
7	Veluwe
8	Overijssel
9	Gelderse Achterhoek
10	Zeeland
11	Noord-Brabant
12	Limburg

Charts in large booklet form, size 20in × 13in, with the legend printed in English and Dutch are available for:—

1803	Westerschelde
1805	Oosterschelde En Veerse Meer
1807	Grevelingen, Krammer, Volkerak en Haringvliet, Hollandsch Diep
1809	Nieuwe en Oude Maas, Dordsche Kil, Amer, Brielse Meer
1810	Ijsselmeer
1811	Waddenzee (Westblad)
1812	Waddenzee (Oostblad)

all of the above publications, from the *Almanak Voor Watertoerisme* to Chart 1812, are obtainable from ANWB, Wassenaarseweg 220, The Hague. Dutch charts and almanacs are also obtainable from Kelvin Hughes Ltd., 145 Minories, London EC3.

If you propose cruising to Holland through the inland waterways of France and Belgium you will not need any advance planning, for the French Permis de Circulation is no longer required and the Green Card (Passeport du navire étranger) is no longer obtainable in advance but issued by French Customs at your port of entry.

If you are not staying in Belgium for more than two months you do not have to register your boat. You simply report to the first

Bureau de Perception des Droits de Navigation to fill in a declaration of entry.

Full details appear in *Through the French Canals* and in the Belgian Canals section of this book.

Enkhuizen, bordering the Ijsselmer.

7 In the Waterways of Holland

The Uniform System of Buoyage in Holland employs the Cardinal on the sea and the Lateral in the rivers and lakes. Allow me to say that you should not be abroad in your boat if you do not understand and recognise the Uniform System of Buoyage, a description of which appears in the *Mariners' Handbook* obtainable from your Chart Agent. Diagrams of both systems and descriptive words, in Dutch, also appear in Vol. 1 of the *Almanak voor Watertoerisme*.

When the navigable channel is not in the middle, beacons along the shores show that the channel is on the same side as the beacons; painted red, white and blue these baskets, or beacons, are fixed to high poles. When two of differing heights are seen close together they are acting as leading marks, (when one is lined up behind the other), to indicate the direction of the channel.

Triangular frame beacons simply mark the ends of the small dykes set at right angles to the shore, the point upwards indicating Starboard and the point downwards indicating Port.

In the smaller waterways perches are used to indicate the channel when necessary.

There is an International Classification of Waterways according to size: —

	Length	Width	Draft	Height	Load
Class I	38m 50	5m	2m 20	3m 55	300 tons
Class II	50m	6m 60	2m 50	4m 20	600 tons
Class III	67m	8m 20	2m 50	3m 95	1,000 tons
Class IV	80m	9m 50	2m 50	4m 40	1,350 tons
Class V	95m	11m 50	2m 70	6m 70	2,000 tons plus

A number of maps show which waterways are which class. Since this book is intended for the cruising yachtsman whose craft will almost certainly be smaller than the smallest class shown above, no attempt has been made to indicate the classification of the waterways in the Cruise Routes in the second half of the book except for the height and draft. Any craft of less than 21m 50 L.O.A. and 4m 50 beam could negotiate *all* of the Cruise Routes subject to the draft and height limitations shown at the head of each route; in most routes the L.O.A. and beam are greater.

As has been mentioned, the size of the waterway is not necessarily an indication of the amount of traffic that it carries.

Regarding the draft column it will be appreciated that some of the waterways, the rivers for instance, will have varying depths but where there is a tidal rise and fall (as much as 2m) the depth shown is the least depth. You will note, I am sure, that depths in this book are shown in METRES as they are on the Dutch CHARTS of the coast, Zeeland, the Ijsselmeer and Wadden Zee. On Dutch WATERKAARTS the depths and other dimensions of the rivers, canals and lakes are shown in DECIMETRES.

On the *charts* the soundings, in metres, are reduced to mean lower low water springs and heights, in metres, are heights above mean highwater.

On the *waterkaarts* you will see depths expressed as NAP plus a figure; you must obviously have a norm in waterways of varying depth and the NAP is this norm. It is an abbreviation for *Normaal Amsterdams Peil.*

Tide tables and some tidal constants appear in Vol. 2 of the *Almanak voor Watertoerisme.*

Tidal influence goes as far as Vreeswijk on the Lek and Zaltbommel on the Waal and the speed of the current is between 2 and 4 mph.

Where lake permits are required—they are obtainable locally—these lakes are coloured yellow on the waterkaarts; waterways closed to all craft are shown in purple on the waterkaarts.

The waterkaarts also show heights of bridges, whether lifting or fixed, dimensions of locks and positions of yachthavens. Extracts from waterkaarts in the Cruise Route Section show the water routes through towns. Where a Cruise Route passes through a town it shows the name of the waterway leading in to the town and the name of the waterway leading out but not the routes in the town itself because these, and alternatives, are clearly shown in the waterkaart extracts. To describe the routes and alternative waterways through towns would require another book and anyhow, you are in safe hands with the waterkaart as your guide and your selection of a route through a town is a matter of personal choice.

At major *road* crossings of waterways the name of the waterway is given, the notice boards being of similar and recognisable style.

In the Dutch official records every waterway in Holland has an official number but since these numbers are not shown in the waterkaarts there is no point in quoting them in this book.

For the cruising yacht there are no special problems about navigation in relation to the avoidance of commercial shipping (all of which will be larger than ones own craft), because the rules can be summed up in five words, 'KEEP OUT OF THE WAY'.

Where there are speed limits (there are none on the big rivers), you will obviously take the speed of other craft as a guide. A reduction of speed at bridges is expected. The speed limits are not imposed only out of consideration for other waterway users but to safeguard the banks from your wash. The speed limits for canals are clearly signposted along the banks and range from 6–15km per hour, depending upon the size of the canal.

On the big rivers the speed and size of passing craft raises such a wash that you cannot leave anything of value free-standing. Even the bother of having to secure everything is not so tiresome as the suction exerted by large vessels passing close to you and drawing you in towards them in alarming fashion. If there was no rule obliging you to keep out of the way you would quickly learn to keep *well* out of the way as a matter of self-preservation.

The Waal is called the 'motorway' of rivers because of the heavy Rhine traffic it carries to Rotterdam. More peaceful are the Lower Rhine, the Gelderse Ijssel and the Maas.

In dodging other craft take particular care before deciding to pass behind tugs, sometimes towing barges so far behind them that, at first sight, they appear not to be connected. The red and white towing flag that should be worn by both is not always clearly visible.

The rules require you to keep out of the way of commercial shipping but what about the situation when you meet other craft of your own size? Encountering other pleasure craft the following rules apply and they will not be wholly unfamiliar to you:—

Approaching each other on opposite courses both alter course to starboard.

Sailing craft have priority over motor craft.

When converging and crossing, the craft which has the other on her starboard side gives way; if both are sailing on different tacks the starboard tack gives way to the port tack; if both are sailing on the same tack the windward boat gives way.

No manoeuvre is permitted that will require another vessel to alter course or reduce speed.

At junctions the boat in the main channel has right of way; when channels are of equal importance the crossing rule applies.

In passages so narrow that only one boat can proceed, the boat proceeding with the current has priority; in slack water sail has priority over power; a sailing boat that can pass the narrows without changing tack has priority over other sailing boats that are not running free; when both can pass the narrows without changing tack the boat with her sail or boom to port has right of way. You may overtake provided that the overtaken vessel can hold her course.

One of the 'big ship' rules of interest is the 'blue flag' rule mentioned in my previous books. A heavily laden vessel having, by reason of draft, to follow the deep water channel whichever side of the waterway this takes him, will fly a blue flag when he is on his 'wrong' side. Normally he is on his right hand side of the river, of course, and so are you. When he puts out his blue flag on his starboard side he comes over to your side of the channel and other shipping approaching him, as you are, must pass him on his blue flag side. But the rivers are so wide in Holland that you hold your course and stay where you are; the deep laden vessel needs so much depth that there will be plenty for you between him and your river bank. In a narrow waterway you would, of course, alter course to pass on the blue flag side.

You will probably hear blue flag vessels sounding twice on their siren to approaching vessels who will make a similar reply. They are simply confirming to each other that the blue flag change of course is understood. Flashing lights are used instead of blue flags at night when, I sincerely hope, you will be safely snugged up in your berth. Perhaps I should enlarge upon this.

When in the big rivers do make sure of finding a stopping place for the night well before dark. Once darkness descends shipping appears to assume twice the volume, twice the size and twice the speed of day; navigation lights, bridge lights, shore lights join forces to bewilder you. You hear monstrous engines pounding towards you and presently a black mountain of a hull glides by;

you look up and see a nonchalant little man high up in the wheelhouse urging his ware-house-sized vessel swiftly ahead into the black night. You should get off the rivers in good time before night falls. On some waterways there is no movement at night.

While it is perfectly safe to hold your course and keep going when meeting 'blue flag' vessels you must make a distinction in respect of passenger steamers that may be coming in to the bank to land passengers. No problem of understanding arises; if a passenger steamer is slowing down it is likely to be going into a landing stage and you will soon see it and act accordingly.

Ferries are a different matter, crossing continually from bank to bank you must judge the best moment to pass them.

The large, vehicle-carrying ferries, independently manoeuvring under their own power, will stop for ships but will not want to stop for you. With the smaller ferries it is simply a matter of judgement and consideration but it is also necessary to determine, as you approach, what type of ferry it is. Some are drawn across on wires stretched from bank to bank, the wires only dropping out of your way when the ferry reaches the bank; on others the cable drops down in front of, and behind, the ferry as it moves across.

Another type of ferry found on the smaller rivers is what is known as the pendulum ferry, so called because it is secured to a long wire that is anchored upstream in the middle of the river, the ferry swinging from bank to bank on this wire like a pendulum. The wire on which it swings is supported above water on two small boats that obviously swing to and fro with the wire. The third boat, furthest upstream, to which the wire is secured, is anchored. (Buoys are sometimes used instead of small boats.) When you approach a pendulum ferry you obviously cannot go to that side of the river where he is, or is going, and you will know that a wire passes between him and his topmost stake-boat. Swinging from bank to bank he is closing each half of the river in turn.

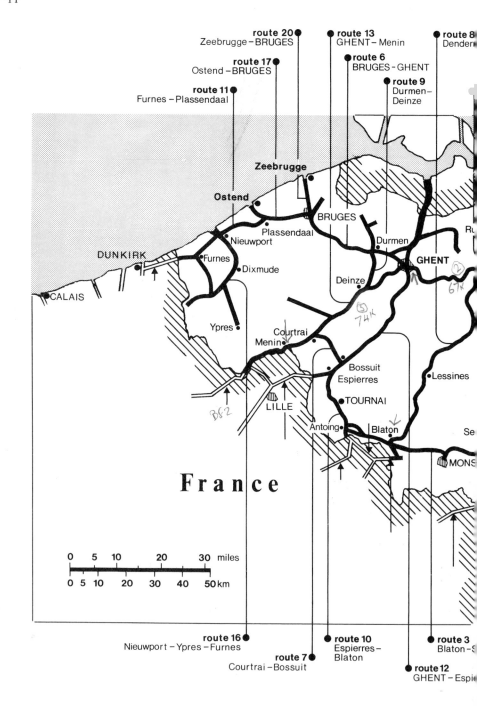

route 20 ●
Zeebrugge – BRUGES

route 13 ●
GHENT – Menin

route 8 ●
Dender

route 17 ●
Ostend – BRUGES

route 6 ●
BRUGES – GHENT

route 11 ●
Furnes – Plassendaal

● route 9
Durmen –
Deinze

Zeebrugge

Ostend

BRUGES

Plassendaal

Nieuwport

Durmen

DUNKIRK

Furnes

GHENT

Dixmude

CALAIS

Deinze

Ypres

Courtrai

Menin

Bossuit

Espierres

Lessines

LILLE

TOURNAI

Antoing

Blaton

MONS

France

| 0 | 5 | 10 | | 20 | | 30 | miles |
| 0 | 5 | 10 | 20 | 30 | 40 | 50 | km |

route 16 ●
Nieuwport – Ypres – Furnes

route 10 ●
Espierres –
Blaton

route 3 ●
Blaton –

route 7 ●
Courtrai – Bossuit

route 12 ●
GHENT – Espie

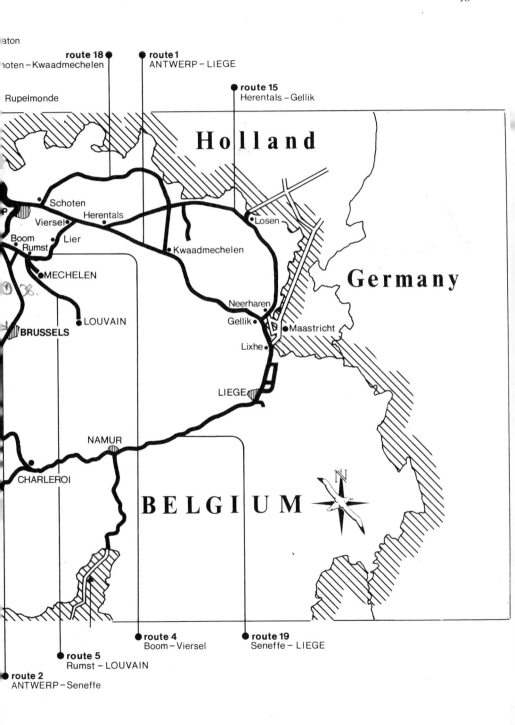

aton

route 18 ● ● **route 1**
ioten – Kwaadmechelen   ANTWERP – LIEGE

● **route 15**
Herentals – Gellik

Rupelmonde

H o l l a n d

Schoten
Viersel ● Herentals
● Losen
Boom ● Lier
Rumst ● Kwaadmechelen

Germany

MECHELEN

Neerharen
● LOUVAIN   Gellik ●
BRUSSELS   ● Maastricht
Lixhe ●

LIEGE

NAMUR

CHARLEROI

B E L G I U M   N

● **route 4**   ● **route 19**
Boom – Viersel   Seneffe – LIEGE

● **route 5**
Rumst – LOUVAIN

● **route 2**
ANTWERP – Seneffe

Alphabetical list of place names with some alternatives—and appropriate route numbers

Alphabetical list of place names (continued)

9 Belgian Route Detail Section

Wester-Schelde to Antwerp

Admiralty Chart 120

From the North Sea up the well buoyed Schelde estuary it is 89 kilometres to Antwerp.

If you contemplate sailing up you should bear in mind that an average of nearly fifty ships a day use this waterway.

When you have passed through the extensive dock and port installation areas the buildings of the city come into view; you

Antwerp.   *Photo Fotowerken Frans Claes*

should then prepare to stand by for 'entering harbour' stations because, just after the right-hand bend ahead, and on your right-hand side, is the Yacht Haven.

The Imalso Yacht Harbour is one of the best in Europe. It is closed off from the Schelde by a lock gate which is open from about two hours before high tide to about two hours after. It is non-tidal in the harbour where the maximum draft is 2,6om.

Near the entrance you can obtain petrol, diesel and water.

Electric power is available, also slipways and winter stowage up to 40 tons.

Watch for the signals before entering or leaving harbour.

All Antwerp clubs welcome members from other 'properly affiliated' yacht clubs.

The Canal Albert, Route 1 next page, leads out from the Straatsburgdok.

The approach to Antwerp.

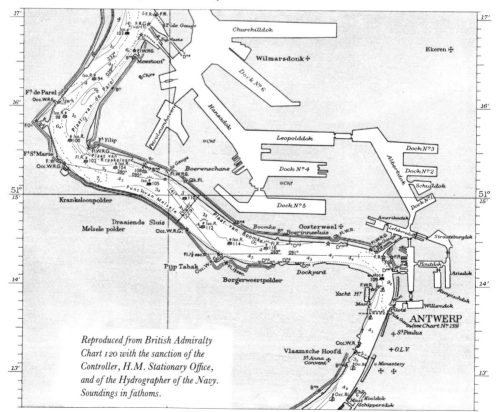

Reproduced from British Admiralty
Chart 120 with the sanction of the
Controller, H.M. Stationary Office,
and of the Hydrographer of the Navy.
Soundings in fathoms.

Route 1 **Antwerp to Liège**

Distance   136kms
Number of locks   6
Minimum height above water   5,25m
Minimum depth of water   2,80m
Maximum LOA   136m
Maximum beam   13m
*See page 197 ref. De Rouck Map Nos.

	Kms	*Locks*		*De Rouck Map No.*
CANAL ALBERT			**ANTWERP** (pop: 675 000). Capital of the province. Second largest city in Belgium. One of the greatest ports in the world, receiving over 16 000 ships a year. 30 miles of quays, 25 berthing docks, 3500 acres of port installations. Famous diamond centre. Fine city, splendid shops. Museums: Van Eyck, Memlinc, Metsys, Rubens, Van Dyck, Jordaens, Van der Weyden, Hals, David, Fouquet, Rembrandt, Hobbema, Titian, Teniers, Martini, Bouts, Fra Angelico, Brueghel, Pourbus, Ingres, Ensor, Broederlam. Arms, carriages, lace, chasubles, furniture, flags, china, pottery, sculpture, textiles, ceramics, gold and silverware, 15th, 16th, and 17thC jewel cases. Model ships, sailing ships, steam ships, small boats, Chinese junks and sampans, exotic miniature boats, navigational instruments; the beginnings of the science of navigation with instruments of torture, dark cells and oubliettes referred to in official publication as an 'alliance between the maritime and the military art'. Printing history. Botanical garden. Zoo (one of the biggest in the world). Many gardens and parks. 13thC Notre Dame Cathedral. 16thC Town Hall. Tourist Office: 19 Suikerrui. Yacht Clubs: Royal Yacht Club of Belgium, Thonetlaan, 133. Antwerp Yacht Club, Bredabaan, 117.	49
(LEFT CANAL DE DESSEL PAR TURNHOUT A SCHOTEN)	6		**WETSCHOT**	49
	3		**WIJNEGEM.** Fast developing industrial centre. One of the oldest towns in Belgium. 15thC miraculous statue of Our Lady. Part Renaissance Pulhof Castle. Part 17thC Kijkuit Castle with Egyptian pavilion.	49

	Kms	*Locks*	**Route 1**	*De Rouck Map No.*
CANAL ALBERT	8		**MASSENHOVEN.** Small village. Some industry. Malicious gossip, which alleged that on Christmas Day flies were put into the currant-bread there instead of currants, was the reason why the inhabitants received the nickname of *Vliegen-stovers* (fly stewers). 18thC Castle of Massenhoven.	49
	2		**VIERSEL.** Small village on the King Baudouin Motorway. 14thC Castle of Hovorst.	49
(RIGHT Canal Nète)	5		**GROBBENDONK.** Important and picturesque tourist centre on the confluence of the Kleine Nète and the Aa. Frankish origin main square. Village of diamond workers.	49
	5		**HERENTALS.** Picturesque holiday site. 15thC Gothic St. Waudru's Church, fine reredos. 14thC Town Hall. Pilgrimage for motorists on St. Christophe's Day, 3 June.	49
(LEFT Canal Bocholt-Herentals)		1		
	6		**OLEN.** Pleasant small town on the Baudouin Motorway. Industrial surroundings, factories, tall chimneys.	49
(From RIGHT River Nète)	6		**STRELEN**	49
	7		**ZITTAART.** 17thC Chapel. Windmill.	49
(LEFT Canal de Dessel à Kwaadmechelen)	5	1	**KWAADMECHELEN**	67
	8		**BERINGEN.** Small mining town.	67
	8		**BOLDERBERG**	67
	2		**STOCKROOIE**	67
	7		**HASSELT** (pop: 40 000). Capital of Provincie Limburg. Lovely old facades. 11thC St. Quentins Cathedral. Provincial museum. Mid-Lent Carnival parade; every seven years parade of the giant *Langeman* and distribution of pea and bacon soup. Syndicat d'Initiative: Town Hall. Hasselt Yachting Club, Grote Markt 37.	67
	2	1	**GODSCHEIDE**	67
	6	1	**KLEIN LANGERLO**	67

	Kms	Locks	Route 1	De Rouck Map No.
CANAL ALBERT		1		
	13		**GELLIK**	67
		2	**LANAKEN**	67
(LEFT Canal de Briegden à Neerharen)	6		**VROENHOVEN**	67
	11		**LANAYE**	67
	4		**LIXHE**	51
(LEFT Canal de Haccourt à Vise)	4		**HACCOURT**	51
	5		**VIVEGNIS**	51
	3		**HERSTAL** (pop: 30 000). Industrial town. National munitions factory.	51

Liège.   *Photo Collection Office du Tourisme Ville de Liège*

			De Rouck
	Kms Locks	**Route 1**	*Map No.*
CANAL ALBERT merges	1	**KING ALBERT STATUE** on Ile de Monsin,	51
with RIVER MEUSE		marking the start of the Canal Albert.	
	1	**LIEGE** (pop: 405 000). Industrial centre and art	51

LIEGE (pop: 405 000). Industrial centre and art city, situated at the confluence of the Meuse and the Ourthe. Gateway to the Eastern Ardennes. Place St. Lambert with great courtyard encircled by sixty columns, all different. Museums, archaeology and applied art among the richest in Belgium; Arms museum with more than eight thousand small firearms. Museum of Walloon life. Gothic St. Pauls Cathedral. Parks, gardens; winding and picturesque streets of Faubourg d'Outre-Meuse. 'Across the Meuse' festivities 15 August. Tourism Office: 5 rue Général Jacques. Yacht Club de Liège, Quai de Rome 58.

Route 2 **Antwerp to Seneffe**

Distance	105kms
Number of locks	12
Minimum height above water	3,70m
Minimum depth of water	1,90m
Maximum LOA	81,60m
Maximum beam	10,50m

			Re Rouck
	Kms Locks		*Map No.*
RIVER SCHELDE		**ANTWERP**	49
(tidal)			
	4	**HOBOKEN** (pop: 30 000). Originated about 1100. The name comes from 'hoge beuken'—tall beeches, which grow there in abundance. Important industrial town: shipyards, metallurgy, the chimneystacks of the silver plant are 383ft high.	49
LEFT into RIVER	15	**RUPELMONDE.** Chief claim to fame as birthplace of Mercator who was also imprisoned here in an old manor house, the remains of which can still be seen.	49
RUPEL (tidal)			
RIGHT into CANAL DE	5	**NIEL.** Attractive small town despite the fact that it produces about 200 million bricks annually. Also shoes, bicycles and small boats.	49
BRUXELLES A RUPEL			
	1		
	5	**BOOM.** Another important brick making town in	49

Antwerp, the Schelde. *Photo by courtesy of the Belgian State Tourist Office*

			De Rouck
	Kms Locks	**Route 2**	*Map No.*

CANAL DE BRUXELLES A RUPEL

BOOM (continued)
a setting of chimneys, claypits and piles and piles of bricks. The basis of this world-wide brick industry was laid in 1235 by the monks of the Abbey of St. Bernard. For more than 600 years the method of production remained unchanged, all work being carried out by hand. Mechanisation was first introduced in 1868. Excursions are now arranged to the brickyards! The people of Boom are known as *hondefretters*—dog-eaters, a memory of World War I famine.

4   1   **TISSELT.** Industrial town. Factories producing cement, asbestos-cement and cellulose; some of them announce that they welcome visitors.   49

3   **KAPELLE-OP-DEN-BOS.** Agricultural and industrial centre.   47

6   1   **NIEUWENRODE.** Small agricultural village.   47

7   **VILVOORDE** (pop: 35 000). A large industrial centre specializing in metal manufacture, chemicals, flour milling and coke ovens. 14thC Notre-Dame Church. Restaurants specialize in horse-steak. Information Office, Town Hall.   47

Kms Locks	Route 2	De Rouck Map No.
8	**BRUSSELS** (pop: 1 200 000). Capital of Belgium and of Provincie Brabant. Royal residence. Gay city with many contrasts, old buildings and picturesque streets side by side with modern blocks, noisy avenues and neon lights. Heart of the city is the Grand-Place, surrounded by the lofty towers of the Town Hall, the King's House and the ornamental Guild Houses. Spacious boulevards, fashionable shops and restaurants. Museums contain artistic treasures too numerous to mention. Royal Palace open to the public from 22 July to 13 September. The oldest citizen is Manneken-Pis, the work of the sculptor Duquesnoy. Musical Instruments Museum. 13thC Gothic St. Michael Cathedral. Tourist Office: 4 rue St. Jean. Brussels Royal Yacht Club at 1 chaussée de Vilvorde, with a large private dock containing mooring facilities for 100 visiting yachts, 3 cranes with a lifting capacity of 15 tons, club-house with bar and restaurant open daily from 0900 to 2300, telephone facilities (number 16.48.28), toilets, fresh water, fuels, shops within half a mile.	47

CANAL DE CHARLEROI A BRUXELLES

3

Kms Locks	Route 2	De Rouck Map No.
9	**RUISBROEK**	47
2		
7	**HALLE.** Pretty little town; art and pilgrimage centre. 15thC miraculous Black Virgin given to the town by Elisabeth of Hungary. 16thC Basilica of Our Lady in Baroque style. Fine collection of sculptures. 15thC font (Tournai art). Effigy of the French Dauphin, son of Louis XI. Renaissance Town Hall. Horse procession, Easter Monday.	47
1		
3	**LEMBEEK.** Somewhat scattered village noted for the Château of Lembeck, a vast construction in local quarry stone, built in 1618; near the picturesque windmill of Saintes. Famous military march of infantry and cavalry on Easter Monday.	47
3	**CLABECQ**	47
1		
3	**OISQUERCQ**	47
2		

The Ronquières Sloping	9	**RONQUIERES**	55
Lock will raise you 220ft			
up an inclined plane			
1432m long.			
	9	**FELUY.** Remains of two medieval castles.	55
	5	**SENEFFE.** A nautical centre with an officially sponsored sailing school. Beautiful castle, 1760.	55

Route 3 **Blaton to Seneffe**

Distance	51kms
Number of locks	10
Minimum height above water	3,70m
Minimum depth of water	1,90m
Maximum LOA	40,80m
Maximum beam	5,20m

	Kms	*Locks*		*De Rouck Map No.*
CANAL DE BLATON A ATH		1	**BLATON**	55
LEFT into CANAL NIMY A BLATON	6		**VILLE-POMMEROEUL**	55
	3		**HAUTRAGE.** There is a small British war cemetery here.	55
		1	**TERTRE**	55
	4		**DOUVRAIN**	55
LEFT into CANAL DU CENTRE	3	1	**GHLIN**	55
	3		**NIMY.** Nearby memorial (on the Railway Bridge) to the Royal Fusiliers.	55
RIGHT to MONS	1		**MONS** (pop: 28 000). Capital of the Borinage. Old mansions, monuments, uneven streets provide a harmonious if somewhat rigid charm. Intellectual and artistic centre. Museums; archaeology, fine arts, ceramics, numismatic, Mons life and, of course, war (1914–18 and 1940–45). St. Waudru	55

			De Rouck
Kms Locks		**Route 3**	*Map No.*

Collegiate Church 1450. Underground prison, 1512. Shrine of St. Waudra sewn in a deer skin; 'Golden Car', splendid gilt coach used to carry the shrine through the town during the famous Trinity Sunday procession and Battle of the Lumecon. Try the local cheese tart. Office du Tourism, 20 Grand Place. Yacht Club: Club Nautique de Mons Borinage, Rue du Fish Club 85.

	1		
CANAL DU CENTRE	7	**OBOURG.** Nearby memorial (at the station), to the Middlesex Regiment.	55
	2		
CANAL DU CENTRE	3	**HAVRE.** Ruined castle of the Dukes, 1603. St. Martin's Church, 1569. Bon-Vouloir Chapel, 1625. Gothic Chapel of St. Anthony en Barbefosse, 16thC.	55
	2		
	4	**THIEU**	55
	3 (hydraulic lifts)		
	4	**HOUDENG-AIMERIES**	55
	2	**LA LOUVERIE.** Important industrial borough. Municipal museum. Mid-Lent carnival. Syndicat d'Initiative, 31 rue Albert 1er.	55
	1	**HOUDENG-GOEGNIES**	55
LEFT CANAL DE CHARLEROI A BRUXELLES	9	**SENEFFE**	55

Route 4 **Boom to Viersel**

Distance 32kms
Number of locks 2
Minimum height above water 1,95m
Minimum depth of water 1,30m
Maximum LOA 81,60m
Maximum beam 10,50m

	Kms	*Locks*		*De Rouck* *Map No.*
RIVER RUPEL			**BOOM**	49
	5		**RUMST.** Although a largely agricultural area, the brick making industry is in evidence with six brickyards. Small boats are also made here.	49
LEFT into RIVER NETE	8		**DUFFEL.** A flourishing place in the 16thC, renowned for its woollen fabrics from which comes the word *induffelen*, to clothe in warm Duffel cloth; thus the origin of the Duffel coat. Vast aluminium plant, paper mills. Ter Elst Castle on the river bank.	49
	7	I	**LIER** (pop: 30 000). Art town and tourist centre. Noted for Zimmer Tower with astronomical clock with fiftyseven dials. Lier is the home town of the watchmaker Zimmer, also the painter Opsomer whose paintings and mementoes may be seen in the Opsomer Museum. Toeristisch bureau, Stadhuis, Grote Markt.	49
	4		**EMBLEM.** Small agricultural village in a region of meadowland and marshes. Also known as the Village of St. Gummarus; this saint is thought to have been born here at the beginning of the 8thC.	49
Joining CANAL ALBERT	8	I	**VIERSEL**	49

Route 5 **Rumst to Louvain**

Distance	28kms
Number of locks	5
Minimum height above water	6m
Minimum depth of water	2m
Maximum LOA	54,50m
Maximum beam	8,25m

	Kms	Locks		De Rouck Map No.
RIVER RUPEL RIGHT to RIVER DYLE			**RUMST**	47
	1		**WALEM**	47
STRAIGHT ON CANAL DE LOUVAIN A LA DYLE (LEFT River Dyle RIGHT River Senne)				
		2		
	5		**MECHELEN** (pop: 65 000). Former capital of the Netherlands and ancient ecclesiastic capital of Belgium. With its gabled 17thC houses it is an attractive city. Noted for lace making and, more recently, furniture and brewing. 15thC Cathedral tower dominates the city. Fine Grote Markt with Spanish style houses.	47
	8		**HEVER**	47
		1		
	5		**BUKEN**	47
		2		
	5		**HERENT**	47
	4		**LOUVAIN** (pop: 34 000). Attractive old Flemish town, best known for its Roman Catholic university and Gothic architecture. 15thC Stadhuis. 15thC St. Pieter's Church. Important textile centre. Badly damaged in both world wars.	47

Route 6 **Bruges to Ghent**

Distance	43kms
Number of locks	1
Minimum height above water	4,50m
Minimum depth of water	2,10m
Maximum LOA	62m
Maximum beam	8,25m

	Kms	Locks		*De Rouck* Map *No.*
GHENT OSTEND CANAL		1	**BRUGES** (pop: 120 000). Famous art town and popular tourist centre. Capital of the West Flanders Province. Episcopal see. Reputed to be the best preserved medieval city in Europe. Known as 'The Venice of the North'; many canals, winding streets, gabled houses, hump-backed bridges, legendary swans. Museums: Van Eyck, Van der Weyden, Van der Goes, Memlinc, Hieronymus Bosch etc; Flemish lace. Oldest Town Hall in Belgium, 1376. 12thC Basilica of the Holy Blood, 13thC Gothic Notre-Dame Church. Tourist Office, Markt 1.	52
	3		**STEENBRUGGE**	52
	3		**OOSTKAMP**	52
	5		**BEERNEM**	52
	2		**ST. JORIS**	52
	2		**BUNTELAAR**	60
	1		**AALTERBURG**	60
	9		**BRUGGEWYK**	60
(Junction RIVER LYS)	5		**DURMEN**	60
	4		**LOVENDEGEM**	60
	4		**VINDERHOOTE**	60

	Kms	*Locks*		*De Rouck Map No.*

GHENT OSTEND CANAL 5

GHENT (pop: 250 000). Capital of the East Flanders Province. Second port of the country. Art town, tourist and University centre. Despite its textile industries, Ghent remains the 'City of Flowers' with picturesque horticultural gardens and fields of flowers. International flower show held once every five years, 1975–80 (*Floralies*). Flower parade first Sunday in September every year except in *Floralies* year. Castle of the Counts, built in 1180, and modelled on the Crusaders' fortresses in Syria. 15thC Town Hall. Museums with Flemish, Dutch, English, French, German, Italian, and Spanish works; fine Hieronymus Bosch. 13thC St. Bavon Cathedral. Tourist Office: Borluutstraat 9. Yacht Clubs: Royal Belgian Sailing Club, Drabstraat 12a; Royal Yacht Club Gent, Eilanderskaai 9.   60

Big changes are in progress in the waterways of Ghent, the intention being to replace the narrow and meandering waterways (however picturesque), with the Ghent Belt-Canal; the possibility of converting the old waterways to subways may become a complete reality. Already closed to shipping are the following waterways: Ketelvaart; Leie, from Recollettenbrug to Krommewalbrug; Canal Brugge–Ghent, between Verbindingskanaal and Leie; Neerschelde.

(right) Ghent. *Photo Stad Gent Toerisme*

Route 7 Courtrai to Bossuit

Distance	16kms
Number of locks	11
Minimum height above water	3,50m
Minimum depth of water	1,80m
Maximum LOA	38,70m
Maximum beam	5,16m

	Kms	*Locks*		*De Rouck Map No.*
CANAL DE BOSSUIT A COURTRAI			**COURTRAI** (pop: 45 000). Attractive town with wide boulevards. World centre of flax industry. Mainly industrial. 14thC Broel Towers, guarding the banks of the Lys, were part of the defences of the castle. 16thC Town Hall. 13thC Notre Dame Church. 14thC Chapel of the Counts of Flanders (Van Dyck's 'Raising of the Cross'). 15thC St. Martin's Church. Carillon of 55 bells. Tourist Office: Town Hall.	52
		2		
	1		**STACEGEM**	52
		4		
	6		**ZWEVEGEM** (pop: 10 000). Small industrial town.	52
	2		**KNOKKE**	52
TUNNEL (600m long. Wait for permission to enter. Lights needed.)		1		
	6	5	**BOSSUIT**	52

46. The Broel Towers, Courtrai. (Not the main Channel.)

Route 8 **Dendermonde to Blaton**

Distance	88kms
Number of locks	35
Minimum height above water	3,70m
Minimum depth of water	1,90m
Maximum LOA	41,20m
Maximum beam	5,20m

Kms	Locks	Route 8	De Rouck Map No.
RIVER DENDRE		**DENDERMONDE** (pop: 10 000). Quiet little town. Town Hall, Cloth Market, and Belfry, 14thC. Basilica and Abbey of Benedictines. 14thC Notre Dame Church. Cavalcade and cortege of the Giants on 15 August. Tourist Office: Town Hall.	60
5	3 1	**DENDERBELLE**	60
8		**AALST** (pop: 45 000). City of art, capital of the Dender country, ancient city of Flanders. The Aalst carnival was a great event in the Middle Ages. Festivities start on Quinquagesima Sunday with a cavalcade; the following day people dressed with astonishing masks invade the town and onions are thrown from the top of the belfry into the crowd in the Market Place below. The carnival reaches its climax on Shrove Tuesday with burlesque fancy dresses. 15thC St. Martin's Church with 16 chapels and 23 altars, remarkable paintings including Rubens, de Crayer. Tourist Office: Town Hall.	60
2	1	**EREMBODEGEM**	60
4	1	**TERALPINE**	60
3		**DENDERLEEUW**	60
3		**OKEGEM**	60
4		**NINOVE** (pop: 12 000). Matches are manufactured here. 14thC Town Gate. 17thC Church notable for Baroque furniture.	60
4	1	**NEDERSTRAAT**	60

	Kms	Locks	Route 8	De Rouck Map No.
RIVER DENDRE		1		
	8		**IDEGEM**	60
	2		**SCHENDELBEKE**	60
	4		**GERAARDSBERGEN** (pop: 10 000). Ancient little town engaged in the manufacture of matches. 15thC Collegiate Church of St. Barthelemy with Rococo truth pulpit. Fountain of Manneken-Pis (a copy presented by the City of Brussels). Procession with Giants in August.	60
		2		
	6		**LES-DEUX-ACREN**	55
		1		
	3		**LESSINES** (pop: 10 000). Important crushed stone quarries. 14thC St. Peter's Church. Gothic Tournai chancel. Our Lady of the Rose Hospital, 1242. Penitents Procession on Good Friday. Syndicat d'Initiative: Flobecq, Ellezelles.	55
		1		
	4		**MOULIN**	55
		2		
LEFT into CANAL DE BLATON A ATH	7		**ATH** (pop: 11 000). Busy industrial town; built in 1168 to defend Hainaut against Flanders and fortified in the 17thC by Vauban. 17thC Town Hall. 'Parade of the Giants' on the 4th Sunday in August. Syndicat d'Initiative: Hotel de ville.	55
		4		
	3		**MAFFLES**	55
		2		
	3		**ST. MARTIN**	55
		1		
	3		**LADEUZE**	55
		4		
	4		**BELOEIL.** Castle of the Princes of Ligne; has been in the possession of the princely family of Ligne for five centuries. Living museum of mementoes of the Ligne family. Fine collections, Beauvais tapestries. Grounds and gardens laid out in 17thC; walks, fountains, pools, arbours. Tourist Office: Castle of Beloeil.	55
	2		**LE PATURAGE**	55
		1		
	3		**STAMBRUGES**	55
		2		
	1		**GRANDGLISE**	55
		7		
	2		**BLATON**	55

Route 9 **Durmen to Deinze**

Distance	13kms
Number of locks	1
Minimum height above water	4,75m
Minimum depth of water	2,30m
Maximum LOA	42,20m
Maximum beam	5,40m

	Kms	Locks		De Rouck Map No.
CANAL DE LA LYS			**DURMEN**	60
	3		**MERENDREE**	60
	2		**LANDEGEM**	60
	3		**NEVELE**	60
	3		**MEIGEM**	60
	2	1	**DEINZE** (pop: 6000).	60

This route is included because the section of the LYS from
Ghent to Deinze is sometimes closed during summer months;
it also serves as a short cut from the Ghent–Ostend Canal to
the River LYS. It is not the pleasantest waterway.

Route 10 **Espierres to Blaton**

Distance	48kms
Number of locks	11
Minimum height above water	3,80m
Minimum depth of water	2,10m
Maximum LOA	39,05m
Maximum beam	5,20m

	Kms	Locks		De Rouck Map No.
RIVER SCHELDE/ ESCAUT (RIGHT Canal de l'Espierres)			**ESPIERRES**	55
	2		**WARCOING**	55
	2	1	**PECQ**	55

			De Rouck
Kms	*Locks*	**Route 10**	*Map No.*
	11	**TOURNAI** (pop: 35 000). A Frankish town and	55

Tournai.   *Photo by courtesy of the Belgian State Tourist Office*

RIVER SCHELDE/
ESCAUT

TOURNAI (continued)
Bishopric it is, with Tongeren, the oldest town in
Belgium. Art town and tourist centre. Dominated
by its cathedral with five towers, one of the finest
buildings of Western art (reliquary St. Eleuthere).
Eight churches, four chapels, Bishop's Palace,
Cloth Hall, Town Hall, almshouses, belfry,
ramparts (11th and 13thC), Henry VIII Tower,
the Pont-des-Trous, six museums, numerous
Roman remains. The two oldest examples of
Romanesque middle-class houses, 1175–1200.
Renaissance houses, many Louis XIV buildings.
'The Procession of the Plague', one of the richest
and loveliest religious events in the country, takes
place on the first Sunday in September.
Tourist Office: Halle-aux-Draps, Grand-Place 56.
Yacht Club: Tournai Yacht Club, Rue de la
Mernière 74.

	3		**CHERCQ**	55
		1		
	4		**ANTOING.** 14thC Town Hall. Neo-Gothic Castle of the Princes of Ligne; double row of ramparts dates from 12thC, entrance fortress from 15thC, dungeon 15thC. Lapidary museum.	55
LEFT into CANAL	6			
NIMY A BLATON		8		
	7		**CALENELLE**	55
	7		**PERUWELZ.** Industrial town. Marble quarries.	55
(LEFT Canal de Blaton				
à Ath		1		
	6		**BLATON**	55

Route 11 Furnes to Plassendaal

Distance	31kms
Number of locks	3
Minimum height above water	4,20m
Minimum depth of water	1,90m
Maximum LOA	45,10m
Maximum beam	6,35m

	Kms Locks			*Re Rouck Map No.*
CANAL DE			**FURNES** (pop: 10 000). Many remains and examples of two centuries of Spanish occupation. Remarkabie Grand Place, 15thC Gothic St. Walburgis Church, 16thC Flemish Renaissance Town Hall, interior richly decorated, Cordova leather, tapestries; 14thC Spanish Officers' House, 15thC St. Nicholas Church. Famous procession of the Penitents on the last Sunday in July. The majority of the penitents cover their heads with a cowl, carry a heavy cross on their shoulders and walk bare footed. Tourist Office: Town Hall.	52
NIEUWPORT A				
DUNKERQUE				
		1		
CANAL DE		3	**KOKSIJDE.** Quite seaside resort. Immense dunes. Archaeological museum. 'Homage to Flemish Painters' Parade last Sunday in August.	52
NIEUWPORT A				
DUNKERQUE				
		3	**WULPEN**	52
		4	**OOSTDUINKERKE.** Noted for Shrimp Festival Parade penultimate Sunday in June.	52
		1		

Kms Locks	Route 11	De Rouck Map No.
1	**NIEUWPORT** (pop: 7000). Seaside resort and fishing harbour. Beautiful beach, wooded sand dunes, pier. Grand Place in Flemish style; town hall and communal museum; market place; sluices and fishing harbour. Impressive monument of King Albert overlooking the historic sluice gates. Tourist Office: Town Hall. Yacht Club: Havengeul 2.	52

CANAL DE NIEUWPORT A PLASSENDAAL

4	**RATTEVAAL**	52

Yacht harbour, Nieuwport.   *Photo Nieuwport Tourist Office*

3	**SLIJPE**	52
3	**LEFFINGE**	52
4	**SNAASKERKE**	52
1 5	**OUDENBURG**	52
1	**PLASSENDAAL**	52

Route 12 **Ghent to Espierres**

Distance	60kms
Number of locks	6
Minimum height above water	3,90m
Minimum depth of water	2,10m
Maximum LOA	125m
Maximum beam	14m

	kms	*Locks*		*De Rouck* *Map No.*
RIVER SCHELDE			**GHENT**	60
		2		
	8		**ZWIZNAARDE**	60
	9		**EKE**	60
	3		**GAVERE**	60
		1		
	2		**ASPER**	60
	4		**NEERWELDEN**	60
	4		**EINE** (pop: 4000). Large textile village.	60
		1		
	4		**OUDENARDE** (pop: 22 000). A quiet town, enlivened by the weekly market on Thursdays and the beer festivals in summer. Oudenarde is famous for its beer. A city of art, gateway to the Flemish Ardennes. 16thC Gothic Town Hall. Romanesque style Cloth Hall. Adriaan Brouwer Beer Festival in the Market Place at the end of June. Cortege of the Giants in September. Syndicat d'Initiative: Town Hall.	60
	11		**BERCHEM**	60
		1		
	7		**ESCANAFFLES**	52
(From RIGHT Canal de	2		**BOSSUIT**	52
Bossuit à Courtrai)		1		
	6		**ESPIERRES**	52

Route 13 **Ghent to Menin**

Distance	74kms
Number of locks	3
Minimum height above water	4m
Minimum depth of water	1,90m
Maximum LOA	42,20m
Maximum beam	5,37m

	Kms	Locks			De Rouck Map No.
RIVER LYS			**GHENT**		60
				The section of the River	
	11		**ST. MARTENS**	Lys from Ghent to Deinze	60
		1		is sometimes closed during	
	14		**ASTENE**	summer months, in which	60
				case ROUTE 9 may be used.	

St. Martens.

Photo by courtesy of the Belgian National Tourist Office

	Kms	Locks	Route 13	De Rouck Map No.
RIVER LYS	2		**DEINZE**	60
(From RIGHT Canal de la Lys)				
	4		**GRAMMENE**	60
	3		**MACHELEN**	60
	5		**OESELGEM**	60
	6		**ST. BAAFS-VIJVE**	60
	3		**WIELSBEKE**	52
(RIGHT to Roeselare)				
	3		**OOIGEM**	52
	1		**DESSELGEM**	52
	1		**BEVEREN**	52
	4	1	**HARELEEKE.** Flax and tobacco growing district. 18thC Church. Romanesque tower.	52
(LEFT Canal de Bossuit à Courtrai)				
	4		**COURTRAI**	52
	3		**POTTELBURG**	52
	4		**LAUWE**	52
	6	1	**MENIN** (pop: 22 000). Industrial town at the end of the Menin Road of World War I fame, recalling Hellfire Corner, the gas attacks of 1915, Clapham Junction, Inverness Copse, Dumbarton Lakes, Black Watch Corner. Nearby cemetery and memorial (Household Cavalry).	52

Route 14 **Ghent to Rupelmonde**

Distance	67kms
Number of locks	o
Minimum height above water	4,35m
Minimum depth of water	1m at LWS (tidal)
Maximum LOA	—
Maximum beam	10m

	Kms	Locks		De Rouck Map No.
RIVER SCHELDE			**GHENT**	60
		1	**GENTBRUGGE**	60
	8		**MELLE.** Noted for its Begonia Gardens and Horticultural College.	60
	6		**WETTEREN** (pop: 20 000). Textile industries. Extensive nurseries.	60
		4	**SCHELLEBELLE**	60
		3	**UITBERGEN**	60
		1	**WICHELEN**	60
		8	**SCHOONAARDE**	60
		7	**DENDERMONDE**	60
(RIGHT River Dendre)		9	**BAASRODE.** Ancient ship-building town.	60
		5	**ST. AMANDS**	60
		1	**MARIEKERKE**	60
(LEFT River Durme)	5			
		4	**TEMSE** (pop: 15 000). Boasts the largest bridge in Belgium, yet the lowest on the Schelde. Industries include textiles, potteries, building of caravans and boats.	60
		5	**RUPELMONDE**	60

Baasrode.

Photo G. Barbaix

Route 15 **Herentals to Gellik**

Distance	99kms
Number of locks	10
Minimum height above water	4,55m
Minimum depth of water	1,90m
Maximum LOA	50m
Maximum beam	7m

Route 16 Nieuwport–Ypres–Furnes

Distance	104kms
Number of locks	6
Minimum height above water	2,50m
Minimum depth of water	1,80m
Maximum LOA	40,85m
Maximum beam	5,15m

	Kms	*Locks*		*De Rouck* *Map No.*
RIVER YSER (LEFT *Canal de Nieuwport à* *Plassendaal)*			**NIEUWPORT**	52
		1		
	7		**SCHOORBAKKE.** Key point in World War I.	52
	4		**TERVATE**	52
	6		**DIXMUDE** (pop: 4000). Rebuilt after its destruction in 1914–18. Town Hall with local museum. Yser Tower and Gate of Peace built in honour of the Flemish soldiers who fell in World War I. Museums and panorama from the tower, 220ft. Old preserved trench known as the 'Bowels of Death'.	52

Nieuwport Yacht Club.

	Kms	*Locks*	**Route 16**	*De Rouck Map No.*
RIVER YSER	7		**KNOKKE-BRUG**	52
LEFT CANAL DE L'YSER A IEPER	3		**DRIE-GRACHTEN**	52
	5	1	**STEENSTRAAT**	52
	8	1	**BOEZINGE.** Marked the boundary of the British Front in World War I.	52
	1		**DOLMEN**	52

Boezinge lock.   *Photo Ypres Tourist Office*

	Kms	Locks	Route 16	De Rouck Map No.
CANAL DE L'YSER A IEPER	10		**YPRES** (pop: 19 000). The very heart of the 'Ypres Salient', 1914–18. British and French military cemeteries, war memorials. Rebuilt, Ypres has retained the character of a medieval town with its ramparts and moats. On the market square the Cloth Hall, together with the Belfry, makes one of the finest examples of a secular building in the Gothic style. The Nieuwerck, 1640, Collegiate Church of St. Martin, Meat Hall, Templar's House (Post Office), Merghelynck Mansion of interest. On the second Sunday in May, the 'Cats' Feast' attracts thousands to Ypres. The main feature is the throwing of cats—live ones in olden days, toy stuffed ones today—from the top of the belfry. Tourist Office: Town Hall.	52
Return to RIVER YSER LEFT	3	1	**LABIETTEHOEK**	52
	3		**FINTELE**	52
RIGHT CANAL DE LO	2		**LO.** 15thC Town Hall. 14thC Town Gate. 15thC Convent containing collection of church art.	52
	4		**FORTEM**	52
	6		**KORTEMILDE**	52
	8		**FURNES**	52

Route 17 **Ostend to Bruges**

Distance	23kms
Number of locks	2
Minimum height above water	4,50m (at Bruges)
Minimum depth of water	2,10m
Maximum LOA	62m
Maximum beam	8,25m

	Kms	Locks		De Rouck Map No.
CANAL D'OSTEND A BRUGES		1	**OSTEND** (pop: 57 000). 'The Queen of the Seaside Resorts'. Port of Dover–Ostend lines. Splendid beach. Fishing and yachting harbour. Important fish market. Kursaal Casino. Thermal Institute, Race Course. Aquarium. Parks. Famous Ball of the Dead Rat on the Saturday following Shrove Tuesday. Procession and Blessing of the sea ceremony on the Sunday following 28 June. Tourism Office: Wapenplein 6. North Sea Yacht Club, Montgomerykaai 1.	52
(From RIGHT Canal de Nieuwport à Plassendaal)	21		**PLASSENDAAL**	52
		1		
	2		**BRUGES**	52

Route 18 Schoten to Kwaadmechelen

Distance	82kms
Number of locks	10
Minimum height above water	4,50m
Minimum depth of water	1,90m
Maximum LOA	50m
Maximum beam	7m

	Kms	Locks		De Rouck Map No.
ANAL D'ANTWERPEN A TURNHOUT			**SCHOTEN.** Noted for the international folk dance festival that takes place in the park of the Schoten Chateau in July.	49
		6		
	8		**ST. JOB-IN-T-GOOR**	49
		3		
	9		**ST. LENAARTS.** Interesting churches and collection of vestments.	49
	5		**DE MEIR**	49
		1		
	4		**BEERSE.** Small brick-making town.	49
	8		**TURNHOUT** (pop: 37 000). Lively industrial town. Many picturesque sights. Palace of Justice, ancient Castle of the Dukes of Brabant. 15thC Church St. Pierre. Syndicat d'Initiative: Town Hall.	49
	8		**RAVELS**	49
	5		**ARENDONK**	49
(Junction with Canal Bocholt-Herentals)	16		**DESSEL**	49
Continuation CANAL DE DESSEL A KWAADMECHELEN	8		**BALEN.** Wooded area, thatched farm-houses.	49
	6		**OLMEN**	49
	5		**KWAADMECHELEN**	67

Route 19 **Seneffe to Liège**

Distance	139kms
Number of locks	23
Minimum height above water	3,70m
Minimum depth of water	1,90m
Maximum LOA	85,11m
Maximum beam	11,50m

2

			De Rouck
Kms *Locks*		**Route 19**	*Map No.*
RIVER SAMBRE		(from HAM-S-SAMBRE)	

Kms	Locks		Map
11		**FLOREFFE.** Picturesque district. Ancient castle. 12thC Church. Military March of St. Peter on the first Sunday after 29 June.	57
	1		
2		**FLORIFFOUX**	57
	2		
10		**NAMUR** (pop: 33 000). Very old town situated at the confluence of the Sambre and the Meuse. Much destroyed during its numerous sieges, almost entirely rebuilt in the 18thC. St. Aubin's Cathedral and St. Loup's Church examples of Baroque architecture. Archaeological Museum. Diocesan Museum. Military Museum. 'Lilliput' miniature village nearby on the road to Marche. Teleferique aerial trip, 62 cabins each carrying two persons 400ft above the Meuse valley. Tourist Office: 2a Place de la Gare.	57
	1		
RIVER MEUSE 8		**MARCHE-LES-DAMES.** Superb rock formations mount guard over the Meuse between Namur and Andenne. It was on one of these peaks, at Marche-les-Dames, that King Albert I fell to his death on 17 February 1934 while on a solitary rock-climbing expedition; a cross has now been erected on the exact spot.	57
	1		
2		**NAMECHE**	57
4		**SCLAYN.** 11thC Church.	57
	1		
5		**ANDENNE** (pop: 8000). Picturesque surroundings. Romanesque Church. Fountain of the Bear 17thC, Fountain St. Begge 1637.	57
	1		
5		**GIVES**	51
	1		
2		**BAS-OHA**	51
4		**HUY** (pop: 14 000). In the narrow alleys of Huy Peter the Hermit preached the First Crusade in 1095. Art town, holiday and tourist centre. 13thC Collegiate Church, 13thC St. Mort's Church, 14thC St. Mengold's Church, Franciscan Friary with tomb of Peter the Hermit who died at	51

Kms	*Locks*	**Route 19**	*De Rouck Map No.*

HUY (continued)
Huy in 1115. *Telepherique des Vallees*, the largest cable car in Belgium.

	I		
5		**AMPSIN**	51
4		**OMBRET-RAUSA**	51
	I		
12		**RAMET**	51
9		**LIEGE**	51

Liège.   *Photo by courtesy of the Belgian National Tourist Office*

Route 20 **Zeebrugge to Bruges**

Distance	12kms
Number of locks	2
Minimum height above water	6m
Minimum depth of water	8m
Maximum LOA	97m
Maximum beam	12m

			De Rouck
	Kms Locks		*Map No.*
CANAL DE BRUGES		**ZEEBRUGGE.** The port area is mainly industrial	. 52
A ZEEBRUGGE		but it is also a fishing port, noted mainly for	
		shrimps. There is a good yacht harbour in the	
		Tijdok. Royal Belgian Sailing Club, Alberta,	
		Omookaai.	
	6 1	**DUDZELE**	52
	6 1	**BRUGES**	52

Zeebrugge.

10 Belgium is so compact

It is difficult to understand why this charming little country remains largely unexplored, particularly by the small boat owner and why so few people know anything about Belgium.

'Belgium did you say?'

Most people look nonplussed, their mental filing cabinets struggling to produce the barest outline: 'A new country, of course; divided between the Walloons and the Flemish; Belgian coalfields; war cemeteries; Ypres and Mons and Mademoiselle from Armentieres; quite nice at Ostend if you like that sort of thing; the Ardennes; not a very big country; there is NATO now, of course; and the Common Market. . . .'

Belgium is, indeed, a small country. In fact it is not easy to register its smallness in readily understandable perspective. To say that it is only half again as large as Wales, or a 346th part of Europe, does not seem to make much impression; but when you consider that a cruise across the widest part of Belgium would be a shorter journey than the distance up the Seine from Le Havre to Paris you begin to appreciate the potential of Belgium as an ideal cruising area.

Belgium is so compact. You can motor your boat to so many fascinating places with so little effort. If you are interested in art you can see Van Eyck at Ghent, Memling at Bruges, Rubens at Antwerp, Breughel at Brussels. Art galleries, museums, castles, abbeys, cathedrals, churches, medieval architecture—something of artistic or historical interest always seems to be within reasonable distance of your waterway.

If you are not interested in art or history you will find much beauty on the rivers and canals with few long stretches between charming little towns and villages. The bigger towns are full of vitality with splendid shops and evidence everywhere of a high standard of living.

There is industry too, of course, for the waterways of Belgium have been a major part of its commercial life for several hundred years. But except in the coal mining regions of the Sambre-Meuse valley the industrial sections do not last for long.

Much can be seen of Belgium in a comparatively short time, not only because of the concentration of interesting places in a small area, but because many waterways have few locks and progress on these is therefore swift. Once past the sea locks at Ostend and Zeebrugge you can cruise straight to Bruges without passing another lock. Through the locks of Bruges you can move on to Ghent unimpeded by locks. There are only six locks in the hundred kilometres of the much used Albert Canal between Antwerp and the Dutch border near Maastricht.

So much to see with so little effort. Brussels, Ghent, Bruges, Antwerp, Mons, Liège, Namur—practically every major town is on a waterway, with distances between measured in hours instead of days, in days instead of weeks.

In fact the only part of Belgium without a navigable waterway is the Province of Luxembourg (not to be confused with the adjoining Grand Duchy of Luxembourg).

To explore the other eight provinces of Belgium you can cruise to Antwerp (capital of Provincie Antwerpen) on the River Schelde or the Canal Albert; to Brussels (capital of Provincie Brabant) on the Canal de Bruxelles au Rupel; to Mons (capital of Province de Hainaut) on the Canal de Mons à Condé, to Liège (capital of Province de Liège) on the Canal Albert or the River Meuse; to Hasselt (capital of Provincie Limburg) on the Canal Albert; to Namur (capital of Province de Namur) on the River Meuse or the River Sambre; to Ghent (capital of Provincie Oost-Vlaanderen) on the Canal de Brugge à Ghent or the River Schelde or the River Lys or the Canal de Ghent à Terneuzen; to Bruges (capital of Provincie West-Vlaanderen) on the Canal de Brugge à Ghent or the Canal d'Ostend à Bruges or the Canal de Brugge à Zeebrugge.

Any place not on the waterway can easily be visited by train for Belgium has more railway per square mile than any other country in the world.

The two most important rivers in Belgium, both flowing from south to north, are the Schelde and the Meuse.

The Schelde rises in Le Catelet-Gouy in Northern France where it is known by its French name, Escaut. It flows over 320kms to

Antwerp, joined by the Leie, Rupel and other tributaries, on the way passing through Cambrai, Valenciennes, Tournai, Ghent, and Dendermonde.

The Meuse rises in Pouilly-en-Bassigny in the southern Vosges mountains in France, not far from Switzerland. It flows over 1000kms to Rotterdam, joined by the Semois, Sambre, and Ourthe, passing through Verdun, Mouzon, Sedan, Mezières-Charleville, Montherme, Fumay, Givet, Dinant, Namur, Huy, and Liège, flowing into Holland at Maastricht where it changes its name to the Dutch Maas.

The coastline of Belgium amounts to only 65kms out of a total of 1140kms of frontiers. In this 65kms there are three 'ways in' to the inland waterways, at Nieuwport, Ostend, and Zeebrugge. At each of these ports excellent facilities exist for visiting yachtsmen. Round the Dutch corner of the Wester-Schelde you can enter the sea lock at Terneuzen and keep your mast up as far as Ghent; or you can carry on past Terneuzen and sail up the Schelde to Antwerp and beyond.

If you needed to put in before Terneuzen there is a pleasant harbour at Breskens with good facilities for visiting yachts.

In addition to those at the entry ports there are yacht clubs on many of the Belgian waterways and these are shown in the appropriate Route Details Sections following.

From France there are eight waterway 'ways in' to Belgium; the Rivers Lys, Escaut, Sambre, and Meuse, and the Canals de Furnes, de Roubaix, Deule, and de Mons à Condé. (The canal from Bergues to Furnes is now closed.) The itinerary generally used from Paris to Brussels passes through the Oise canal to the Sambre, up to Charleroi and through the Charleroi canal (down the world famous Sloping Lock of Ronquières) to Brussels.

From Holland the River Meuse and the Canal Zuid-Willemsvaart are the inland waterway routes.

Although yachting and pleasure boating generally is growing in popularity in Belgium there is virtually no yachting industry there at all. The few Schelde shipyards that built 'one-off' yachts fifty years ago seem to have retired from yacht building in favour of their more enterprising Dutch neighbours.

A feature of Belgian life not fully appreciated by visitors (since eighty-five per cent of them do not venture beyond the seaside resorts), is the dual language situation. A can of beans is *haricots sauce tomate* in one place and *witte bonen in tomatensaus* in another. Of course the Flemish speaking and French speaking areas are defined and, superficially, only seem to acquire significance in the political arena.

Belgium is divided more or less equally between Flemings and Walloons. The Flemish speaking belong to the same race as the Dutch and inhabit the north west (East and West Flanders, Antwerp, Limburg, and northern Brabant). The Walloons in the south (southern Brabant, Hainaut, Namur, Liège, and Luxembourg) resemble their French neighbours. The language frontier, as it is called, is south of Brussels although French is principally used in the capital.

One day, alongside a barge on the Ostend-Bruges canal, the skipper declared almost scornfully, 'Of course I don't come from these parts.' He looked at us as though he expected us to recognize this. 'I come from France.'

'Where in France?' we replied, interested.

'Liège,' he told us proudly.

We had heard that there was no such person as a typical Belgian, as there is a typical Englishman, Frenchman, or Italian. Our skipper's attitude caused us to remember this.

The dual language problem for the visitor is that practically all place names have two names, often alike (*Brussels—Bruxelles*; *Brugge—Bruges*), but by no means always so (*Gent—Gand*; *Kortrijk— Courtrai*; *Leuven— Louvain*; *Liège—Luik*).

Map reading and route planning presents some difficulty on this account and in an attempt to overcome it a list of place name alternatives is given at the beginning of the Route Details Section.

So far as getting around is concerned a great many people all over Belgium speak English and German in addition to French and Flemish.

The Route Map at the beginning of this section and the Route Details Section show the main navigable waterways of Belgium arranged as 20 routes, each connecting from one waterway junction to another. The towns and villages on or near each of these routes are also set out briefly in most cases in this section. Distances and the number of locks are shown, also convenient map references.

For instance, if you plan to enter Belgium at Ostend, Route 17 will describe the route as far as Bruges. Continuing on Route 6 will take you to Ghent; from here you may proceed on Route 14 as far as Dendermonde, turning right here on Route 8, down the River Dendre to Blaton, right on Route 10 to Espierres and right again on Route 12 back to Ghent.

		Kms	Locks
Route 17	Ostend to Bruges	23	2
	Canal d'Ostend à Bruges		
CONTINUE ON			
Route 6	Bruges to Ghent	52	
	Canal de Bruges à Ghent		
CONTINUE ON			
Route 14	Ghent to Dendermonde	38	1
	River Schelde		
TURN RIGHT			
Route 8	Dendermonde to Blaton	88	35
	River Dendre		
TURN RIGHT			
Route 10	Blaton to Espierres	48	11
	River Schelde		
TURN RIGHT			
Route 12	Espierres to Ghent	60	6
	River Schelde		
TURN LEFT			
Route 6	Ghent to Bruges	52	
	Canal de Bruges à Ghent		
CONTINUE ON			
Route 17	Bruges to Ostend	23	2
	Canal d'Ostend à Bruges		
		384	57

In cruising these 384kms and 57 locks you will have explored the dream town of Bruges, known as 'The Venice of the North'; the art town of Ghent, 'City of Flowers'; historic Dendermonde; the art city of Aalst; the old fortified town of Ath; the Chateau of the Princes of Ligne at Beloeil; the cathedral town of Tournai, oldest in Belgium; the ramparts of Antoing; the Belgian city of art, Oudenaarde, gateway to the Flemish Ardennes.

How long this would take you would obviously depend upon how long you wished to spend each day in the active business of cruising, but it could certainly be regarded as a leisurely fortnights' cruise.

Study of the Route Map will show how many permutations and

combinations of other routes may be planned on these lines.

In order to plan what distance you can cruise in the time you have available you would not be far out if you reckoned upon averaging 3 knots between locks and 30 minutes to pass through each lock. (This is simply a rough average for planning purposes only. At some of the bigger locks a wait of several hours is not uncommon.) Some routes have more locks than others and how many you can manage in a day will depend upon the number of your crew and their agility. We seem to average around twenty locks a day, which is a reasonable target for two people; there will be many days planned when the number of locks to be passed through will not approach this number.

The general speed limit on the inland waterways is 3½ knots. You may see speed boat types exceeding this, but it is likely that they will have obtained special permission to do so on the understanding that their hull form does not cause excessive wash; and then only in certain restricted areas. As usual, common sense is the best regulator. A speed that causes no damage to the banks nor inconvenience to others is the right speed (including fishermen and ladies doing their washing at the river bank). Speed limits in the tidal waterways are higher where necessary for safe manoeuvring, but be guided by the barges in this matter.

In planning your cruise it will pay to consult as many maps and guide books as possible so that you go through, or near, most places of interest. The *De Rouck* provincial maps are so useful for this purpose that the appropriate map numbers have been placed against each place name shown in the Route Details Section. If you write to the local *Syndicats d'Initiative* or *Toeristisch Centrum* of the towns along your planned route (for addresses see the Route Details Section), they will be pleased to send you information regarding items of interest in their area and of events taking place at the time of your proposed visit. Folklore in Belgium is universal and it would be a pity to miss any of the wonderful carnivals.

I have claimed in earlier books that inland waterway cruising is the most delightful experience because it caters for every taste. The active can be as active as they wish and the leisurely as leisurely 'all in the same boat'.

No permit is required to cruise on the Belgian waterways unless your stay extends for more than two months (see chapter on **Planning the Cruise**). You are therefore free to cruise wherever you wish.

The details given against the place names in the **Route Details**

Section are not by any means comprehensive, but it is hoped that the brief data given will arouse your interest sufficiently for you to want to seek further information. I am indebted to my many friends in the various tourist offices for supplying the details shown. At each of the places named, whether described or not, it is understood that at least a shop will be nearby.

No special skill is needed to handle a boat on the Belgian waterways. Any active couple with the intelligence to navigate a car will find no difficulty in handling a motor cruiser. Many thousands of people have enjoyed inland waterways holidays without previous experience.

I do not suggest that anyone without experience should cross the Channel from England to Ostend unaccompanied, however. The North Sea is no place for beginners. Quite apart from the experience needed to follow a satisfactory course there is always a great deal of shipping traffic; at any time of the day or night there will always be ships within view, all going different ways, ahead, astern or crossing.

The shorter journey from Dover to Calais or Dunkirk may be preferred. It will then be a simple matter to cruise up, say the Canal de Furnes into Belgium but it should then be borne in mind that French entry papers will be required (see *Through The French Canals*, Nautical Books).

11   Planning the Belgian cruise

The time you have available will determine the extent of your cruise; if you have several periods of limited time you may consider leaving your boat in Belgium ready for your next cruise. This is not so inconvenient as it sounds if you plan accordingly, putting suitcases and kitbags onboard that would not otherwise be there. You can hire a 'drive yourself' car from a number of points in Belgium, and load up alongside, leaving the car at Ostend.

Junctions . . . in a field. River Lys and Canal de la Deule.

There is no time limit on cruising in Belgium in the sense that there is in France. Pleasure craft do not need to obtain a permit in advance. These remarks apply to craft over 3 tons; pleasure boats of less than 3 tons are only admitted into the canals and navigable rivers 'on sufferance', to quote the Regulations which go on to say (about boats of less than 3 tons), 'their passage may be proscribed by the Chief Engineer-Director who holds jurisdiction over those stretches of waterway where their presence might inconvenience shipping'. Addresses of the Engineers/Directors are given at the end of this chapter.

Although your cruise in Belgium is not subject to any time limit, you have to come into line with Belgian pleasure craft if your stay exceeds two months; this entails carrying a registration plate at the stern of your boat. These plates are personal to the owner and need renewing each year before 1 March (if your boat is remaining in Belgium covering this period, since the plates are of different colour every 'registration year'). They must also be replaced if lost or on change of ownership of the boat.

There are two kinds of registration plates (*plaque d'immatriculation*); *oval* in shape for craft under 3 tons, and *oblong* in shape for

... in a town. River Lys and River Schelde. *Photo Stad Gent Toerisme*

craft over 3 tons. (In some places craft with *oval* plates are expected to be ashore every night, so make sure that you get the right one.)

Plates may be obtained at the local office of the Inspector of Navigation or at a Pay Office of Navigation Dues.

Coming into line with Belgian pleasure craft will also mean that the name of your boat must be shown in letters 8cm high on each side of the bow, the name of the home port in letters 8cm high on the stern, and, above or below this, the name of the owner in letters 4cm high.

If your stay in your boat in Belgium does not exceed two months, your craft does not require these formalities. You should carry onboard a copy of the rules governing navigation for pleasure on Belgian inland waterways. They are set out in a brochure called *Dispositions réglementant la Police et la Navigation*, which also contains useful information such as tables of distances, ports, timetables of locks and bridges. It may be obtained from: The Editor, Etablissements d'Imprimerie Dantinne, Stree, Province de Hainaut, Belgium.

About the only thing required of you by the Belgian Customs is to prove that your craft is not being brought into Belgium for sale (in which case triptyques, carnets de passage en Douanes and other involvements with Customs arise). This proof must take the form of a membership card or letter to the owner from a recognized yacht club, establishing that the craft is registered or based abroad.

At your entry port into Belgium you report to the first *Bureau de Perception des Droits de Navigation* to fill in a declaration of entry. Navigation dues will make little impression on your small change but do not destroy the receipt as it will be required later, sometimes at locks. On leaving Belgium you report to the last *Bureau de Perception* to sign a declaration of departure. If the date of this last visit, compared with the date of the first receipt mentioned above, reveals that your stay in Belgium has exceeded two months you become liable to pay the 'registration plate' dues already outlined.

Of course you will ensure that each person onboard is in possession of a valid passport. A list of persons onboard is sometimes required when passports are presented. If your stay in Belgium extends to over three months your passport then needs to be supplemented with a Provisional Stay Visa.

You are free to cruise any waterway in Belgium and there is no compulsory pilotage. You will obviously get much greater enjoyment out of your cruise if you plan it in detail in advance. Use the Route Map in conjunction with the **Route Details Section**; this also gives the appropriate *de Rouck* map number from which you can note places of interest that lie near your proposed route.

The junctions on the Route Map are the meeting places of waterways; it does not necessarily follow that there will be a village or a town there too, nor even a single building. For instance, the junction of the River Lys and the Canal de la Deule is shown as at Deûlemont since it needs to be identified. In fact there is nothing but fields, trees, and cows at the actual junction; Deûlemont is a short walk away.

There is much beauty on the waterways of Belgium.

12 In the waterways of Belgium

On arrival at your Belgian port of entry you are required to present yourself at the first Collector's Office of the Rights of Navigation where a declaration of entry will be issued to you.

Having satisfied the few entry formalities, the next pleasant and prudent step will be to make the acquaintance of the local yacht

Yacht Basin, Ostend.

club. The location of these is shown under each appropriate place name in the **Route Details Section.**

Advice on the unstepping of the masts of sailing yachts will be available, for facilities exist at all entry ports. Allow a day or so for this and for the subsequent lashing and stowing of rigging and gear.

There will also be fuel and water available, and you should top up to capacity before setting off on your inland waterway adventure into Belgium.

Most of the yacht clubs in Belgium are pleased to offer free mooring for the first day or so, but enquiries should be made at the outset.

The usual ways in from Nieuwport, Ostend or Zeebrugge are simple enough, all being straight canals once the sea lock is passed. Not a great deal of barge traffic will be encountered.

Yacht Club, Nieuwport.

You will find that barge traffic may well be moving at times when you will not want to be disturbed and, on busy waterways, it will pay to seek an out of the way spot for the night, if one can be found.

It will not be wise to secure to a barge for the night without first ascertaining what time it is leaving in the morning. It is unpleasant to be awakened, in darkness, by the sound of your warps arriving on your deck, and frightening to feel your boat lurch free in the wash of a powerful screw.

As might be expected, some waterways carry considerably more barge traffic than others. Where there is heavy barge traffic there will be a number of areas of waterside industrial concentration, and in these areas you will not want to linger long.

Since commercial use of the waterways is expressed in tons carried it will come as no surprise to learn that the Schelde estuary to Antwerp is the industrial leader in the waterborne tonnage league. But one ship may equal twenty or more barges and it is a noble river.

Next in order, but carrying less than half the tonnage of the

Straight Canal from Zeebrugge.

Schelde, is the canal from Terneuzen to Ghent. Not even the most ardent lovers of Belgium would claim any beauty for this waterway. One might think of it as a quick way in through the back door to Belgium, and backyards are seldom attractive.

Only fractionally less traffic is carried on the Albert Canal from Antwerp to Hasselt, but probably in a greater number of barges because it is a smaller waterway. Surprisingly enough the Canal Albert passes through pleasant wooded countryside. The few locks are large and power-operated so that it is possible to cruise the length of it in two or three days. But there will not be many times when you will have this waterway to yourself, in fact there will be few moments in a day when you will not be sharing it with other traffic, all forcing ahead on their urgent business.

If a cruise from Antwerp to the Meuse is contemplated, a detour can be made on the Canal Bocholt-Herentals and the Canal Zuid Willemsvaart (Route 15), with less than a third of the Albert Canal barge traffic. But on rejoining the Albert Canal at Gellik, the next heaviest traffic section builds up with the joining in of barges from the Maastricht direction, and this comparative density continues to a point beyond Liège at Hermalle S/Huy.

Antwerp to Brussels on the Canal de Brussels au Ruppel is next in order of barge traffic, but below Brussels, the Canal de Charleroi à Brussels carries only a third of the barges entering Brussels from Antwerp.

The Albert Canal. All forcing ahead on their urgent business.

From Ghent down the River Escaut is next busiest, followed by that section of the Meuse between Hermalle S/Huy and Namur.

Lowest in the barge traffic ratings is the Canal de Brugge à Ghent and the River Schelde from Ghent to Rupelmonde; almost equally matched by the Canal Bocholt-Herentals already mentioned.

In the waterways not mentioned you will not be unduly disturbed.

Compulsory pilotage is not necessary on any of the waterways of Belgium; indeed there are few problems. You will know that you should keep to the right and proceed at a reasonable speed. If you come across a barge being towed from a tow-path you will obviously pass on the side opposite to the tow. It will also be obvious that such a tow-path is no place to tie up for the night.

In all cases where they are applicable the Rules of the Road must be observed and it is hoped that no yachtsman would consider making the crossing to Belgium unless he was familiar with them.

You will be passed by, and will pass, other traffic without comment. On some of the narrower waterways do not expect approaching barges that are heavily laden to go over to their right hand side of the channel for they will probably be drawing a great deal more than you; and if you come up astern it is as well to stop in some interesting spot to allow him to get ahead. The regulation requiring a prolonged warning blast by the overtaking vessel is not always observed, although it should be, even when there is plenty of water.

Keep a good look out for ferries, dredgers and fishermen and give each a good blast on your siren to warn of your approach Do not tie up by loading and unloading quays, nor by locks; also avoid securing on bends in the waterway.

Bridges that open, (also some locks), display Stop and Go lights. Although you will find different patterns and sitings, and sometimes more than one light, the intention of each will be apparent. Obviously RED means Stop and GREEN means Go. RED and GREEN together means Stand By. On sunny days it is sometimes difficult to see the lights when the sun is behind them. Discs are sometimes used by day and lights during darkness or fog. Discs always show RED for Stop, but may show either GREEN or

(left) The Meuse.   *Photo by courtesy of the Belgian State Tourist Office*

WHITE for Go; discs are usually edged with a black band but you will also encounter red discs on a white background and white discs on a green background. If you always stop for red, or red and green together, you will keep out of trouble.

If you see a disc turn from RED do not let go immediately and surge forward as you would in your car at rush hour traffic lights. The disc may stay 'in neutral', showing neither side, which is a signal to stand by.

Where bridges have more than one channel look for a RED signal in the centre of one of the spans; this will obviously be the way you are NOT to go. If there is no such prohibition you will keep to the channel on your right.

A succession of green lights showing on both sides of the channel are there to indicate the width of the channel; often an amber light will be visible over the centre. If a red light shows it means Stop.

Bridge lights, particularly on the busier Belgian waterways, have different patterns at night. If you are cruising for pleasure I strongly

(left) Other traffic . . . Antwerp.   *Photo A. de Belder*   (above) Other traffic . . . Zeebrugge.

recommend that you are safely tied up before sunset. If it is urgent for you to keep moving there will always be other traffic to show you the way.

There is much beauty on the inland waterways of Belgium, much art and history nearby, numerous waterside towns and villages waiting for you to explore. But there is industry too. Plan your cruise with care so that the beauty and interest of Belgium is highlighted in your memory, the industrial scene relegated to the background where it belongs.

Index

Note: An index of PLACE NAMES
appears on pages 31 and 146
An index of Dutch WATERWAYS
appears on page 34